crossing boundaries

crossing boundaries

attraversar confini

edizioni **j**unior

With the contribution of the Emilia-Romagna Region, Department for the Promotion of social policies and educational policies for childhood and adolescence. Policies for immigration. Development of voluntary service, associations and the third sector.

Photo of the Conference of Marina Castagnetti from the Centre for Documentation of Educational Research, Institution of Nursery schools and crèches of Reggio Emilia.

The photos in the "Narrating the possible" section come from the archive of the Centre for Documentation of Educational Research, Istituzione Scuole e Nidi del Comune di Reggio Emilia.

Translations: Pierre Italia s.n.c., Bergamo

Cover photo and graphic design of the Conference: Rolando Baldini and Vania Vecchi

ISBN 88-8434-279-1

© Edizioni Junior s.r.l.
Viale dell'Industria - 24052 Azzano San Paolo (BG)
Tel. 035/534123 - Fax 035/534143
e-mail: edjunior@edizionijunior.it
web site: www.edizionijunior.it

First printing: February 2006

Printing 10 9 8 7 6 5   4 3 2 1
               2010 2009 2008   2007 2006

Printed in Italy
Tecnoprint s.n.c. - Romano di Lombardia (Bergamo)

Presentation

This volume contains the proceedings of the conference held in Reggio Emilia in 2004 entitled "Crossing Borders".
It was a conference on **children's rights** in the world and on the capability of towns to meet these rights with the appropriate services.

A work session, as well as a part of this book, was dedicated to **Loris Malaguzzi**, to his teachings, his capacity to dream and let us glimpse possible futures and to design innovation.
In the work of Loris there were, in the very first place, children and their rights and he invited adults to respect them without any ambiguity. For this reason too, Reggio Emilia with Loris and all those who accompanied him every day in the schools: administrators, teachers, parents, educationalists...has become a privileged meeting place for those who want to experiment education on the side of children.

The network has extended over the years. The friends of always, like the National Group of Crèches, founded in Reggio Emilia with Loris in 1980, have been joined by others in Italy and all over the world who, with headstrong stubbornness, great effort and at times without resources, try to prove that *history can be changed by reclaiming it, starting from the fate of children*.

2004 was an important and delicate date for the nursery schools and crèches of Reggio Emilia: forty years after the first council school, the Robinson school, the local council decided to run the crèches and council nursery schools through the Institution.
Fears... perplexities...new attention... all these emotions swung high and low and they were voiced in the wide corpus of the system of families, personnel and citizens...

The courageous choice was made to tackle the theme **of identity**, giving rise to an itinerary of collective research on the identity of crèches and nursery schools in a period of great change.

Identity between memory and future were the main subjects of study and each crèche and nursery school produced "evidence" of its identity with "historic" teachers, younger teachers, parents who became citizens in the municipal childhood boards (because their children are now grown up) and parents of today who are coping with being a mother or father for the first time.

The issue of memory, at a time like the present, when it seems as though there is room only for the present, is a subject that concerns Italy and other countries, because memory is long and the threads that hold it together must be strong... *silk threads*, Loris Malaguzzi would say.

But at times like this where the future is difficult to imagine, we felt that only by "**crossing borders**" can we try to be prepared with knowledge and skills for the future. Geographical borders and borders of knowledge, divided into fields that are too separate, force us today to illiteracy which is not new.

Each crèche and nursery school worked on producing the seminars, with the sessions of dialogue investigating them in greater depth; they will be mentioned only briefly in this volume.

This volume is published today (February 2006), because since Loris Malaguzzi passed away (in 1994), we feel that the best way to remember him in his city is to present a new project.

This year, the occasion is truly extraordinary: the inauguration of the International Centre, which the city has decided to dedicate to him.

A meeting place and a place of hope for children and adults who still believe that it is possible to imagine places where everything is not standardized, not indifferent and not the same.

Sandra Piccinini
*President of Istituzione Scuole e Nidi
del Comune di Reggio Emilia*

This experience and my account of it have no leave-taking.
If at the end any message is still needed, it is a message of reflection.
I do not know how adult the world of adults really is. I know that the rich, adult world hides many things, while the poor one knows neither how nor what to hide.
One of the things that it hides with the most rigor and callousness is the condition of children. I will refrain from detailing the data about death and desperation.
I know that my account is a luxury. It is a privilege because the children of whom I speak live in the rich world.
But also in this world, deception continues, at times cynical and violent, at times more subtle and sophisticated, laced with hypocrisy and illiberal theories. Deception infiltrates even the institutions of early education.
The continuing motivation for our work has in fact been an attempt to oppose, albeit with modest means, this deception and to liberate hopes for a new human culture of childhood.
It is a motive that finds its origin in a powerful nostalgia for the future and for mankind.

Loris Malaguzzi

from "The Hundred Languages of Children", Ablex Publishing Co. 1993

It is my great pleasure to extend a warm welcome to the speakers and participants of the conference "Crossing Boundaries", from the Municipal Administration of Reggio Emilia, the city where the first Italian Tricolor flag was created and where men and women, forty years ago gave life with great foresight to that extraordinary experience which is today the extensive, high quality network of municipal services for early childhood.

Men and women who, in the midst of all the difficulties of reconstruction following the second world war, chose to advocate the right of children to have quality schooling and a future.

A lovely story which had its beginnings forty years ago, and which has grown and changed in the same way that the city has grown and changed. It is an experience which has accompanied, sometimes even anticipated, the changes inside our community which has not stayed still, but has decided to take up the challenge of modernity in the name of collective interest.

It is an experience which has been capable of producing excellence also after the loss of its most important protagonist, Loris Malaguzzi, pedagogista of international fame and founding father of the pedagogical approach which Reggio Emilia carries forward in encounters and dialogue with the entire world.

As Municipal Administration we have carried out this task with many other partners: Reggio Children, the International Association "Friends of Reggio Children" and starting from this year, with the Istituzione Scuole e Nidi d'Infanzia, the instrumental organisation used by the Municipality for the management of the system of educational services for early childhood in our city.

In the hope that this conference offers each one of you positive opportunities for exchange and sharing on educational strategies for childhood, for sharing with our citizens (as individuals and in organized groups) the ideas and good practice of an educational town which might help local institutions and cities themselves to extend the ideas of democracy and participation, I wish you all a beautiful experience during these days in Reggio, both on a professional and human level, and that you may remember them for years to come.

Antonella Spaggiari
(Mayor of Reggio Emilia from 1991 to 2004)

crossing boundaries

attraversar confini

**The rights and potentials
of children
and adults**

The Mayor of Reggio Emilia, Antonella Spaggiari, confers honorary citizenship on Jerome Bruner (June 1997)

Working for children so that they can enjoy their rights

Jerome Bruner

I'm terribly sorry that I'm not going to be able to be there to celebrate the 40th anniversary of Reggio Emilia municipal preschools. It is occasion in which preschool educators from Italy and all over the world meet to celebrate this fantastic kind of school model, which is based on the idea that you treat three, four and five year olds as if they were people and enter into dialogue with them. Intelligence shows itself in dialogue, and this dialogic intelligence is strictly related to somehow being in the community. In Reggio Emilia, I have even had four and five year olds trying to explain to me why their classes are so interesting, and it is really quite amazing.

However, I realize that it is so important to me that I have seen that town in other respects, I must say it is a town full of a sense of the future.

Its industry, for example, is made up of advanced electronic manufacturing. It does not consist of just manufacturing as such, but also the newest forms of fashion. Max Mara, for example, is based in Reggio Emilia and has stores all over the world. It represents new fashion, not just novelties but honest fashion - I like their style. The other thing I like very much is that when the communities of all over America, like in Colorado or in California, want to set up schools for young children, where do they go for advice? To Reggio Emilia. It's the community that runs these schools. This participation in the community is the most interesting thing, but the danger is that these schools have succeeded so well they risk forgetting their origin.

You know the old proverb that says "the fish will be the last to discover water"? Well, I have a feeling that in Reggio today, they may be taking the city too much for granted. That is something to worry about. I think it is necessary to go back and look at the origin of its history, in order to discover the sense of this today.

Let me just say a little bit about today, about the problems not only in schools but also in cities. I have seen big cities having trouble dealing with the ever-increasing influx of non-EU immigrants. This is not the case in Reggio Emilia: what they have done here is set up a program for receiving and training the immigrants, and even the elderly are part of the program. I keep won-

Jerome Bruner
New York University, USA (video recording)

dering how this city has managed to develop such an advanced kind of social consciousness that is so concerned about problems. This issue is fascinating for us Americans and makes us want to study your history.

I think the history of all of this starts at the time of the French revolution. The people of Reggio were enormously impressed with the revolution and its ideas. They were then under the control of the Estensi family (the Dukes of Modena), but they formed secret "cells" to explore and discuss things like "La déclaration des droits de l'homme" and debated over what were the rights of man. However, their hopes exceeded what was possible at the time. They wanted to have a new kind of world and so they rebelled against the Estensi family. Together with neighbouring cities, they formed a new republic, the Cispadania Republic (this is such an interesting thing: forming a republic with neighbouring cities two to three decades into the 19th century…).

Their hopes exceeded what was possible when Napoleon came to Reggio Emilia; but then Napoleon betrayed their revolutionary ideas, so the exceptional change that everyone was waiting for never happened. Your history has always seen great efforts to achieve autonomy in some way or another, because autonomy is independence. Autonomy is also initiative and determination. Take your theatre for example: the people of Reggio were so determined to have a theatre that eventually the Teatro Valle was built.

Reggio is a small city, but I find its Teatro Valle absolutely astonishing. What we have here is a little opera house, an opera house in Reggio Emilia which I think is more beautiful than la Scala in Milan. This shows the level of quality the people of Reggio expect. To some extent I think that the Duke of Modena, and the other Dukes of Modena along the way, recognized that the only way to keep people under control was to give them quality. But even that never really satisfied Reggio.

In some respects I find Reggio very much like the United States: being a colony is never appreciated. Another episode so typical of this city is when a malaria epidemic breaks out in that region of Reggio Emilia. To deal with malaria, you need quinine, which could have been distributed in the same way as in other cities of the region. But that's not the way you do it in Reggio: what they did was set up the "farmacia", a local pharmacy to be sure that the price was kept down so that nobody could get malaria. I go to the same farmacia today a century later.

There is a special role of women in this approach, and I think this is terribly important. I'm struck by how this sort of rebellion continues with a kind of wanting more independence, even when the war came along and Italy entered the next phase of fascism under Mussolini.

Reggio Emilia probably suffered just as much as any other city from the oppression by the fascist government, because it was under the fascists when it became part of the "Red Belt". I don't know what it meant by the city being radical, but who were the radicals? The radicals were the best families of Reggio Emilia, and even with fascism, there was a period in which there was still a good deal of informal activity and still a lot of labour union activity. A lot was done underground, but the same push for autonomy, which had been so effective in keeping them separate from the domain of the Estensi family and the Dukes of Modena, also kept them independent during the fascist period.

So when the Mussolini period came to an end, there was this tremendous feeling of liberation. There was an industrial renaissance, as well as the beginning of a new cultural activity, like the establishment of museums, the re-establishment of the Panizzi library and so on. This process has continued ever since, and when I come now to Reggio Emilia I find myself surrounded by educated Japanese, Norwegian, Swedish and Dutch, all who have come to see for themselves.

One thing which a lot people do not know about Italy but which I have learnt is the enormous extent of control from Rome over the Ministry of Education and the schools. However, compared to the national control from Rome and this force, there is still a local community control that stimulates people to discuss things.

This is what I mean by autonomy: it is about moving in this direction locally and making people aware of things and taking direct responsibility.

I have observed what happens in those schools: more than 3,000 young children - and I don't know how many families - are directly involved in the education process and in dialogue.

Let me give you an example. They were doing a little exhibit of the way in which shadows are cast with a light behind a stick that casts shadow - if you put it further behind, the shadow changes and so on. The teacher was in a dialogue with a young girl called Gabriella. She asked Gabriella, "Why does the size of the shadow change? You know when you move the light closer to it…", or something like that… Gabriella was trying out different answers and she got a little bit confused, so the teacher turned to the other children and said, "Can somebody help Gabriella"? So the class got into a conversation in which they were all involved. Not only were they trying to solve the problem of cast shadows, but they were also attempting to help somebody who hadn't fully understood it. I sat there amazed. Then the children stopped talking to the teacher and to each other, and started trying to explain to Gabriella what the principle was. That is so typical of the way the city runs. Another time was last summer, when I went to a meeting in which the industrialists of the city were talking about future plans for expanding to Eastern Europe with their products. I got that same kind of sense of talking to each other, with questions like: "How should we…?" and "We have a joint problem…. how do we solve it?"

I welcome all these people from so many different countries. There are something like 800 people at this particular congress, and if I were there, I would welcome you all. But I would also like to give a special welcome to people from other Italian cities, because I think in some way this also represents a sort of a new expression of the Risorgimento, a kind of building up of a culturally responsible Italy – of course I don't mean to be at all denigrating to glorious Malaguzzi.
The establishment of preschools led to what I think was a tremendously important thing. The development of this new, now world-famous nursery school was certainly incredibly innovative, but one of the most important things in this was the entry of women as part of the women's independence movement. I know this was a movement that had tremendous power. Now there are more professions open, there are more women going into medicine, and more are going into law. The same level of specialization of women in teaching is one of the incredible facts.

The rights of children?
There are very many ways in which you can destroy human rights, and I think one of the main findings of the 20th century is that you can destroy the human rights of adults by failing to give them an adequate childhood. I know about this because I was one of those who was "impeded" at the beginning, when I began supporting the new ideas of respect and education of children in America. We succeeded luckily but only just. If you don't give some kind of a start to children, if you have lost your opportunity to develop your mind fully, do you have the right to do whatever you want? What kind of a right is that? It's like saying to somebody: I'll chop off your right hand but I'll make you become a pianist.
Finally, what is interesting to me is that it's not some passion for pedagogy that makes Reggio Emilia - contemporary Reggio Emilia which I know very well - so concerned with these children. Rather, it is the belief that it is essential to guarantee them a life as an effective coping adult.
That is a wonderful reason why philosophy is what it is: each child is autonomous and should be treated as an individual; each child is an artist, each child is a scientist as best they can be... Every child is given an opportunity to grow into effective adults. That to me is the ultimate granting of rights to children: not putting up a sort of a battle saying we are in favour of the rights of children, but doing something so that they can use their rights as well.

Children's rights in Namibia
Do children have rights?

Barnabas Otaala

Introducion

The number of conferences, workshops, seminars and fora in education that take place is quite staggering. Not a week passes without a local, a national, and a regional or international conference on education. I submit that so long as there are educational problems/challenges, so long will conferences, workshops, fora continue to be held; if for no other reason than to reassure ourselves that we are still on the right track.

People everywhere, but particularly in developing countries, are struggling with similar daunting problems: hunger, homelessness, rapid population growth, unemployment, violent crime, poor health, the preventable deaths of millions of children, widespread environmental degradation, and education systems inadequate for countries' needs and people's aspirations.

But the world is at the threshold of a new century, with all its promise and possibilities, with the cumulative experience of reform, and innovation. In the case of children, a number of international events in favour of children have marked the past few years:
1. The Alma Ata International World Health Organization (WHO) Conference which took place in 1978.
2. The Child-to-Child movement was started in 1978, shortly after the Alma Ata Conference which launched the world-wide commitment to spreading the concept of Primary Health Care (PHC), in preparation for the International Year of the Child (IYC) in 1979;
3. The ratification by the United Nations of the Convention on the Rights of the Child in 1989;
4. The passage by the Organisation of African Unity of the African Charter on the Rights and Welfare of the Child;
5. The Jomtien World Conference on Education for All, held in Thailand in March, 1990. One thousand five hundred delegates from hundreds of nations and organisations gathered to assess conditions and develop plans to improve education around the world. The World Conference generated an action

Barnabas Otaala

University of Namibia, Namibia
International Committee World Forum

plan and launched the Education for All movement to meet the basic learning needs of all children, youth and adults in all counties of the world;

6. The World Summit for children in September 1990, which was attended by seventy Heads of State.

In Namibia, we have already made some significant progress both with respect to the implementation of the Convention on the Rights of the Child, and support for early childhood care and development. We now have a National Policy on ECD - an achievement which remains as aspiration and hope for a number of countries in Africa, including those who achieved their independence earlier! The number of ECD centres and enrollments has also increased. But quantitative indices alone are not enough. We must also have our attention directed at the **qualitative** aspects of early childhood care and development.

Children need our special attention more than ever before. With the spreading of HIV/AIDS, children have become more prone to exploitation and misuse of their fragility and defenselessness. Children of whatever age need our continued protection.

In the following paragraphs I will refer to some statements on how we have gone about implementing the Namibia Policy on Early Childhood Development (ECD); I will also refer to how we have implemented the Child-to-Child approaches in Namibia; I will briefly also refer to some evidence-based statements on what child rights mean to a selected community in Namibia - - the Nama of Karas and Hardap regions of Namibia. Finally I will refer to the issues which have brought about a retrogression in our development - - HIV/AIDS - - before making concluding remarks.

Progress in implementation of early childhood development policy

Background

At independence in 1990, Namibia was characterized by extreme disparities in land and property ownership, access to health, education and other social services. Whereas less than 10% of the population owned most of the land and enjoyed a high standard of living, the majority of Namibians lived in poverty with limited access to wealth-generating capital and life sustaining social services. Although the situation has greatly improved in the past 13 years, high unemployment amongst many Namibians continues to keep them in poverty. When put in historical perspective, this situation becomes easier to explain. (Hengari and Zimba, 2003)

At independence, the Government issued a development brief for education, culture and training. Titled *"Towards Basic Education For All"* (1993) the brief identified four tenets which are the cornerstones of Namibia's educational system today - - **Access**, **Equity**, **Quality**, and **Democracy**. A word then about translation of these into the area of Early Childhood Education (ECD).

ECD provision after independence took the form of pre-school and childcare programmes. Most pre-schools promote child development and increase children's readiness for primary school. Centre-based childcare programs for three-to-five year-olds offer educational, health, nutritional, developmental screening and social assistance services. Another form of ECD provision that should be noted is the home-based custodial care that caregivers provide to some children whose parents go to work. (Iithete, et al., 2000).

To capture the attention and support given to children after independence, the following milestones, are worth brief cataloguing.

– Article 15 of the Namibia Constitution is on the rights of children. These are rights to survival, protection and development. In addition, article 20 of the Namibian Constitution provides all children aged 6 to 16 years the right to Basic Education. All these provisions demonstrate, at the legislative level, Namibia's commitment to meeting children's needs.

– On 28th September 1990 the Namibian Parliament ratified the United Nations Convention on the Rights of the Child. In addition to those already mentioned, these were rights to health, education, play, justice, free expression, and protection from violence, abuse, child labour and protection from exploration.

– Namibia contributed to the realization of the 1990 World Summit Goals on the survival, protection and development of children by putting in place in 1991 the National Program of Action for Children in Namibia. This programme was incorporated into the First National Development Plan (NDP 1) (MOHSS, 1999).

– To promote the health of Namibian children, the Ministry of Health and Social Services designed and implemented the Primary Health Care Policy in 1992. This policy put emphasis on nutrition, provision of safe water, basic sanitation, community health education and training, immunization against childhood diseases and on maternal and child health care.

– In 1994, the Namibian government, in collaboration with local NGOs, formed an inter-ministerial task force to develop a National Early Childhood Development Policy. In 1996, this policy was put in place. The main objectives of the policy were to:

- make the public more aware of the importance of creating stimulating and supportive environments for young children;
- clarify the role of government in the provision of early childhood development services;
- consolidate laws and programs related to Early Childhood Development for all children, with emphasis on children living in difficult circumstances and those living in rural areas;
- clarify roles and responsibilities of government, churches, NGOs, CBOs, the private sector, and communities involved in Early Childhood Development programmes;
- propose ways in which stakeholders in the field of ECD can network in support of children and advocate for their rights and needs;
- suggest strategies communities could use to mobilize material and human ECD resources and build capacity to support children optimally;
- to implement the ECD national policy, the Namibian Government established the National Early Childhood Development Committee (NECDC) whose main mandate is to coordinate efforts of all stakeholders in ECD;
- the Namibian Government in 2001 rededicated itself to the Namibian children by declaring 28 September as the day of the Namibian child. (Hengari and Zimba, 2003).

A word about Child-to-Child and some research on children's rights.

Child-to-Child approaches in Namibia

Child-to-Child started as an international programme designed to teach and encourage older children, especially school children, to concern themselves with the health and general development of their younger brothers and sisters and of younger children in their own communities. The programme has grown from a few health messages to be spread by children into a worldwide movement in which children are considered as responsible citizens who, like their parents and other community members, can actively participate in the community and in the developmental affairs of the community.

The approach emphasizes that children need to be accepted as partners to promote and implement the idea of health and well-being of each other, of families, and of communities. In so accepting them, you help them to develop, and the approach enhances their

own worth both in their own eyes, and in those of adults. Hence there is a strong link with the idea of children's rights. You respect partners and you work with them.

The parallel between Child-to-Child and the **Convention on the Rights of the Child** may not be immediately obvious, but the philosophy and work of Child-to-Child is in fact a practical expression of the **Convention's** many provisions which seek to make children **subjects** rather than **objects** of efforts to ensure their survival, protection and development. Articles 5 and 14 of the Convention speak of the evolving capacities of children; Article 12 refers to children's right to express views freely in all matters which affect them; Article 24 obligates governments to "ensure that all segments of society, in particular parents and children, are informed, have access to education, and are supported in the use of basic knowledge of child health and nutrition, the advantages of breast-feeding, hygiene, and environmental sanitation, and prevention of accidents". These extracts from the **Convention** read like guidelines for a Child-to-Child project.

In Namibia Child-to-Child was formerly introduced towards the end of the first year of independence (Mostert and Zimba, 1990), at a major workshop held in Windhoek, with participants coming from health, education, NGOs, and communities. Later a series of workshops was held in both northern and southern Namibia (Otaala, 1994a; Otaala, 1994b). During the workshops teachers and health workers are provided with selected health messages which they can pass on to older children who in turn can pass them on to their younger brothers and sisters, other children, their parents, and the communities from which they come. Selected Child-to-Child activity sheets such as **Playing with younger children**; **Preventing Accidents**; **Road safety**; and **Immunisation** have been translated from English into Oshindonga for use by primary school teachers and children in Owamboland, one of the most populous parts of Namibia.

Currently there is a proposed pilot project to examine the workings of the Child-to-Child approach in colleges of education and selected nearby satellite schools. As a result of the operating and monitoring of this project over a period of time it would be possible to assess better the potential of Child-to-Child approach in health education; the potential of colleges of education in promoting such an approach, and the value of health education as a model for promoting more active, learner-centered, relevant and community related learning in other areas of the curriculum, and within the school as a whole. (Otaala, 1995)

Children's rights

In a 1995 study Zimba and Otaala, among other things, examined Nama childrearing practices associated with selected articles of the Convention on the Rights of the Child, and tried to draw up programmatic implications of these practices.

We observed, firstly that there seemed to be conceptions of children's rights that were consistent with universal understanding. Children's rights to education and good health were, for example, valued by Nama parents in ways similar to those expressed by concerned parents all over the world. However, the Nama families faced considerable hardships in providing for their children's education and medical care. Unemployment, lack of stable incomes and lack of affordable medical schemes were used to explain the hardships. Income generation activities and general community development initiatives appear to present possible solutions to the problems.

Secondly, there appeared to exist conceptions of children's rights that were inconsistent with current global formulations. Nama parent's conceptions of corporal punishment present a good example here. From a non-Nama perspective, it would seem that the endorsement of the use of corporal punishment in the home and at school violates children's freedom from physical and emotional abuse. According to the Nama, this interpretation would be inappropriate. To them, corporal punishment is **one** of the tools available to parents for socializing children into honest, well-behaved, self-disciplined, obedient and reflective individuals. In addition, it helps to produce out of children persons who fear and respect authority. To them, this is important for the maintenance of regulated and ordered social relationships. Our judgement is that this concept conceptualization should be taken into account when championing the cause against child abuse. Obviously, most Nama parents do not perceive any abuse when corporal punishment is intended to create out of children responsible human beings with some realistic understanding of social and emotional connotations of right, wrong, unfair, fair and just actions.

Thirdly, our data revealed contextualized conceptions of children's rights. These were displayed when the consideration of the freedom to make their own choices and decisions regarding entertainment, spending money, friends, schools and churches to attend did not only implicate the social-cognitive developmental needs and welfare of the children but in addition involved matters of safety, security, protection from harm, custom, tradition and social relations with peers and adults. For example, whereas more than half of the respondents thought that adolescents were old enough to exercise the freedom of choosing their own friends, more than a third of them considered this to be in error because to protect them from alcohol and drug abuse, forming anti-social behaviour, bad influence and the misuse of sex, the youth required advice, counseling and guidance from their parents and other adult family members. It appears from this understanding that according to the Nama the exercise of children's rights to free choice and decision making should take into account their **contextualized best interests**. These interests should reflect Nama custom, tradition and contemporary social-cultural, social-economic and community development realities. (Zimba and Otaala, 1995, pp. VIII – IX).

Scope of HIV/AIDS and orphans in Africa

In Africa there are an alarmingly high numbers of children homeless and living on the street. The plight of these children has been a matter of great concern to UNESCO which focuses in part on combating the exclusion of children from any given society. The street children crisis has been deepened by the HIV/AIDS pandemic, which is a formidable challenge and obstacle, not only to the economies of several countries, but also to families and communities in the South African Development Community (SADC) region.

GLOBAL HIV EPIDEMIC

– Since its first documented appearance 20 years ago, HIV has infected more than 60 million people worldwide.
– Globally, there are an estimated 40 million people living with HIV.
– About one-third of those currently living with HIV/AIDS are between 15 – 24 years.

REGIONAL HIV EPIDEMIC

– Sub-Saharan Africa is the region most severely affected by HIV/AIDS:
– 3.4 million new infections in 2001
– 28.1 million people are living with HIV/AIDS regionally.
– HIV prevalence rates have risen to alarming level in Southern Africa.
– Recent antenatal clinic data show that several parts of Southern Africa have prevalence rates among pregnant women exceeding 30%.

Source: AIDS Epidemic Update: UNAIDS/WHO, December, 2001

Sub-Saharan Africa is said to be amongst the most severely affected regions by the HIV/AIDS pandemic. This has contributed to an increase in the number of children living on the street, children living in families with inadequate care and support, and children resorting to high-risk behaviour for their own survival and that of their siblings, such as commercial sex and child labour. As a result, more and more children in the sub-region are being affected by and becoming infected with, HIV/AIDS. This threatens both their health and social acceptability. The chances of these children entering and remaining in school to attain a basic education are thus severely reduced.

	Totale dei bambini con HIV/AIDS viventi	Bambini che hanno perso uno o entrambi i genitori per HIV/AIDS	Morti stimate per AIDS
Botswana	10 000	66 000	24 000
Lesotho	8 200	35 000	16 000
Malawi	40 000	390 000	70 000
Namibia	6 600	67 000	18 000
Swaziland	3 800	12 000	7 100
Zambia	40 000	650 000	99 000
Zimbabwe	56 000	900 000	160 000

Source: Report on the Global AIDS epidemic: UNAIDS/WHO, June 2000

Challenge of "Shame, Discrimination, Stigma" (SDS)

In Namibia's Constitution discrimination on the grounds of colour, religion, sex, place of origin and state of health are prohibited. Many officials preach against discrimination and stigma. Yet, on a daily basis, there are several reports in schools, in communities, and in places of work, where people are being discriminated and stigmatized on the basis of their being affected and infected with HIV/AIDS. AIDS orphans, particularly, have borne the brunt of this "shame, discrimination and stigma" (SDS). Yet in traditional African customs and practices, orphans and other vulnerable children used to be well taken care of, and grew up in a spirit of acceptance.

The most effective health interventions are worthless if they are not used. What is it about our cultures that compels us to overlook a major barrier to improved healthcare: the entwined issues of stigma, discrimination, and shame (hereafter, SDS)?

SDS is such a powerful force that, if there is a chance their conditions would be revealed, people would rather suffer and die, and have their children suffer and die, rather than access treatment that could improve their quality of life and save their lives. Currently, those with any number of illnesses are stigmatized and rejected, as are family members, if those illnesses are made public. People also hide their medical conditions because they fear, oftentimes justifiably, that they will lose friends, jobs, housing, educational and other opportunities, if their conditions are publicly known. The many conditions affected by SDS include forms of cancer, Hansen's Disease, mental illness, mental retardation, tuberculosis, domestic violence, substance abuse and dependence, sexual dysfunction, and sexually transmitted diseases, now most notably HIV disease.

Repeatedly and loudly and for decades, experts at the international level and service providers at local levels have described the powerful forces of SDS. No less a personage than the late Jonathan Mann, then Director of the WHO Global Programme on AIDS, warned the world about SDS in regards to HIV. In 1987, speaking informally to the UN General Assembly, he "identified three phases of the HIV/AIDS epidemic: the epidemic of HIV, the epidemic of AIDS, and the epidemic of Stigma, discrimination and denial". He noted that the third phase is 'as central to the global AIDS challenge as the disease itself'. (cited in Parker et al, 2002)

"Each year, more and more people die from the (HIV) disease and it is the stigma and misinformation around HIV that is killing people," Juan Manuel Suarez de Toro, president of the International Federation of Red Cross and Red Crescent Societies, said in a recent World Red Cross Day message. "people place themselves at high risk from infection or refuse to access treatment rather than face the consequences of social stigma, such as losing their homes, businesses and even their families," he said. (Olafsdottir, 2003)

From the statements made thus far, we can summarise that, there are children's rights recognized in Namibia. They include:
- to give the child the possibility of being heard in any administrative procedure that involves him/her
- to guarantee his/her right to a compulsory basic education, to health services, and to equality regardless of ethnic, tribal or religious origin or gender;
- to provide disabled children with special care and guarantee their access to services;
- to establish a minimum working age and to protect children against exploitation in the workplace and against any other forms of exploitation;
- to protect the family and insure the equality of men and women within the family;

– to protect the child against cultural and social practices that are harmful (e.g., nutritional taboos, female circumcision, early childhood marriage);
– to establish the minimum age of marriage at 18 and to make the recording of marriages compulsory;
– to protect children against recruitment in armed conflict.

This leads me to my concluding remarks.

Concluding remarks

Given what has been said above about the challenges that face us, someone might easily conclude that we have ended with a "paralysis of analysis". I should therefore hasten to echo James Thurber's words: "let us not look back in anger or forward in fear; but around in awareness". In concluding, I want to draw our attention to two key areas, attention to children, and attention to the critical role of education, to which we must pay attention.

Let us remind ourselves of the UNICEF position paper for the World Conference on Human Rights, held in Vienna in June 1993:

"The best interests of the child are universal. They include the right to survival, to healthy development and protection from abuse. These rights are agreed. They are international standards. But what value do they have in a world which turns its back on hunger and want, on torture, rape, and exploitation of children?

Children's lives cannot be put on hold while adult society mulls over its obligations towards them. Public commitments have been made. Treaties have been written and ratified. The time to act is now!"
Also, as I have had occasion to say many time before, in different fora, the survival and protection of children is the responsibility of all of us, individually and collectively, including us the participants at this very important conference, because as Leon Chestang (1974) has aptly observed:

> *"And so I ask, who, if not us, will nurture*
> *our children?*
> *Who, if not us, will protect them?*
> *And who, if not us, will assure them*
> *of their birthright? Who?"*

On education one can say that it holds the key to development, to receptiveness to others, to population control and to the preservation of the environment. Education is what will enable us in Africa especially, to move from a culture of war, which unhappily we know too well, to a culture of peace, whose benefits we are only just beginning to sense. We are prepared to deal with the threats of the past but we are still helpless when confronting the threats of today and tomorrow.

There should be a consensus that time has come to move from discussion to decision, and from decision to implementation. Further delay in tackling the education crisis particularly in teacher education as it exists in each country or region and globally will have a very high cost in both financial and human resource terms.

Dean Acheson, one of the great and witty Secretaries of State in the USA tells about a bright young diplomat who came to him once and outlined a brilliant strategy. The young man ended his presentation by saying, "And with the help of God, we shall carry this through." To this the Secretary responded: "Unfortunately, young man, God doesn't work for the State Department!"

God may not work for African or Reggio Emilia children either: I would hope and pray, however, that **HE** has a watchful eye on their healthy growth and development, under the Convention the Rights of Children, and other provisions, meant to protect our most precious resource, and the future of humanity.

References

GRN (1996). *National Early Childhood Development Policy in Namibia*. Windhoek: GRN.

Hengari, J.U. & Zimba, R.F. (2003) Coordination of Early Childhood Development Policy and Provision in Namibia. Report to UNESCO.

Iithete, I., Haihambo-Muetudhana, C., Hengari, J., Otaala, B. (2000). *In Search of Early Childhood Care and Development (ECCD. Indicators: A Contribution to the EFA 2000 Assessment. The Case of Namibia.* Windhoek: Printech.

Mostert, M.L. and Zimba, R.F. (1990) *Child-to-Child in Namibia*. Windhoek, University of Namibia Printery.

Olafsdottir, S. (2003, May 12). Red cross at Forefront of Fighting Stigma. The Herald. Harare, Zimbabwe. Available at: wysiwyg://11/http://allafrica.com/stories/printable/200305130573.html

Otaala, B. (1994a) *Child-to-Child in Northern Namibia: New* Initiatives. Windhoek, Frewer's Printers.

Otaala, B. (1994b) *Child-to-Child in Southern Namibia*. Frewer's Printers.

Otaala, B. (1995) *The Contribution of Educational Psychology in Africa: The Namibian Case*.

Otaala, B. (1995) *Health Through the School:* A Proposed Pilot Project.

Parker, R., Aggleton, P., with K. Attawell, J. Pulerwitz, & L. Brown (2002, May). HIV/AIDS Stigma and Discrimination: Conceptual Framework and an Agenda for Action. *In Findings from the Field, A Compilation to Date of Publications on HIV/AIDS from Horizons and Partner Organizations:* May 2002. (CD-ROM). New York: population Council.

Zimba, R.F. & Otaala, B. (1995) *The Family in Transition: A Study of Childrearing Practices and Beliefs Among the Nama of the Karas and Hardap Regions of Namibia*. Windhoek. UNICEF and the University of Namibia.

Children's rights in Nepal
Social change in the communities of the poor

Agatha Thapa

It is necessary that I introduce my country Nepal, briefly, so that my presentation becomes relevant to you. It is a land locked country bordered by China on the north and India on the east, south and west. It is a country of Mt. Everest, the himalayas with snow covered peaks. It is also the country of Lord Buddha, the prince of peace. Nepal is a mosiac of geographical, social and cultural diversities.

Today we all have gathered here in this beautiful town of Reggio Emilia, to listen to the voices of children from across the boundaries. We have come to listen to the joys and sorrows of our children. Because, they are the challenges and threats to the knowledge we hold, to the expertise we have, to the discoveries of science and technologies, to the various researches and above all to the civilization of mankind. Whatever good is happening for the children in today's world is very little, compared to large number of children still suffering from lack of education, lack of safe drinking water, mal-nourishment, ill-health and lack of hygienic condition.

Today whatever evil things we hear, we see and we experience, are the consequences of our negligence in the past. As a result, the whole world is suffering from various grievances such as racial discrimination, discrimination against women, economic exploitations, environment exploitaions, conflict between the nations, threats of mass destruction which are our everyday stories and have become today's common issues. Violation of human rights and injustice all over the world are integrated within the system in which we live. Human dignity is not honoured. It is a matter of common concern, that is why we have gathered here to listen to the grievances that have affected not only our present but our future also.

This is the global realities of today. In this context, Nepal has its own constraints. Nepal is one of the poorest countries in the world. Inequitable access to land complicates the dependence of the largely rural population on subsistence agriculture, and has meant a

Agatha Thapa
Seto Gurans National Child Development Services,
Nepal - International Committee World Forum

growing reliance on the cash economy. This means increased migration for men for work, heavier workloads for women and children, and an erosion of traditional family patterns. Internal conflict over recent years has caused even greater hardship for the country's poor.

Mortality and malnutrition rates remain high for young children in Nepal, and their daily care is compromised by the focus on day to day survival. Most disadvantaged families feel powerless to promote their children's best interests and underestimate their capacity to support young children's learning and ability to interact effectively witht the world.

Discrimination against girls and women in Nepal still affects almost every area of their lives – ten girls die for every seven boys, they get less to eat, less health care, less access to school, less chance to play, and less choice in their lives.

Twenty percent of Nepal's children still are not enrolled in school, and the figures are higher for girls and untouchables and other disadvantaged groups, Those children who start school are poorly prepared, and schools are equally unprepared to respond to their needs. Attendance is low, failure is frequent, and repeat and drop out rates are high, especially in the first two years. Problems associated with the transition to school require serious attention. One particular problem is the number of underage children that, lacking care at home, accompany older siblings to school, swelling the population in already overcrowded classrooms.

Discrimination and injustice that I have mentioned above are the barriers that prevent the mankind from the full enjoyment of human life. These barriers must be broken somewhere at one point.

We all desire change but inspite of our effort, the change we expect has been slow and frustrating. We cannot wait any longer. The transformation must begin now and this has to begin with our children. Vision of new world with justice, progress and peace, should take its foundation on the opportunities that we offer to our children today. We are not just talking about the opportunities but we are talking about equal and appropriate opportunities, because these are our children's rights. We all know only a small number of children are getting quality opportunities and a vast number of children are deprived of this right. Of course we know that, all equal opportunities do not bring equal result, because there are many other governing factors which are beyong our control. We are talking about

something that is within our power, that is trying to change the social, cultural, economic, and political context in which we live. We are trying to minimize the negative impact of the present condition on our children.

Early Childhood Development has the power to change the poverty situation in many countries like ours and transform the social structure by changing man's way of thinking, their attitude, hopes and beliefs. Social structure can't be changed, unless the attitude of the people changes. Oppression and exploitation will not change until the attitude of the oppressor as well as the oppressed both changes towards each other. The psychologists say that the development of attitude is rooted during the early childhood. Based on this fundamental truth early childhood development/education must be taken as people's movement for change.

When I mention early childhood development as a mass movement, I would like to introduce you a situation where such a movement is being evolved, aiming a rapid change in the society.

Let me take you to a trip to a little village in Nepal not very far from town. Your journey begins from the capital city of Kathmandu in a local bus. Bus heads towards the east to a district called Kavre. The three hours short journey is extended to almost five hours because of frequent military and police checking, investigating and questioning. The suspicion and insecurity prevails everywhere because of seven years of Maoist insurgency that is going on in Nepal. As you arrive the bank of the river called Roshi, the motorable road ends. After you cross the river, a tough trek begins on the rough path to a steep climbing up the hill. Continuous walking will take you through jungle, fields, barns, orchids, thatched houses etc. You come across men and women washing and bathing near by water sources and streams.You come across children rearing cows and goats and playing happily in the fields. The cow sheds are usually located close to human living to keep the cattles safe from the wild animals. Children and animals are friends and both grow together freely with nature. You will enjoy the simplicity of life.

As you continue your trek you will notice scattered houses here and there over the hills. Now, let me take you to a community of untouchables. Do not be surprised when I say untouchables in your civilized 21st century. How can some human being can be untouchable? Why this discrimination ? But untouchablity is a traditional disease of cast system in nepal. I would like to show you how the ECD movement for social change begins in this particular community. The people are involved in the construction of a one room house for the ECD centre. This is a community which has never been school themselves. How come that they are wanting an ECD program for their children. What brought the change in their thinking and attitude?

Your attention is drawn by the voices of children from nearyby. It is an open field ECD program organized by a trained facilitator who is one of the mothers in the community. She has created a learning environment for children in the open field because construction of ECD centre building is not complete. Children have made their own play areas under the trees, on the slab of stones, constructing their imaginative house with the bamboo blocks, wooden pieces, stones and mud. If you go closer to these children, you will see them involved in life skill oriented activities – traditional weaving, stringing bamboo beads, pasting on leaves, sorting out seeds, stacking size graded bamboo pieces, moulding clay, playing with sand and water. Some are rolling straw balls, some are engaged in throwing and catching straw rings etc. More activities will be added when the house is ready. Grand parents and parents in the neighbourhood are welcome to be a part of an open space ECD program. You may ask what happens on a rainy day? Naturally on such a day, children must stay at home. That is why construction of the centre must complete soon before the rainy season begins.

As you travel further up the hill and move from village to village, you will come across more open space ECD program organized by ethnic community of Tamang tribes. They are very jolly hill tribe with rich culture. Dance and song is the way of their life. They have their own ethnic language and traditional musical instrument. Their economic condition is no better than those of the untouchable community that you have just seen. The source of the curriculum forECD program in this ethnic groups is dance, music, their traditional games and stories. Six ECD model centre are already establised and other four are under construction. The community contributes land, parents contribute bamboos and labour, the community forest contributes wood, the partner INGO (Save the Children-Norway) contributes roof and the government contributes matching fund. District Seto Gurans and District Education Office provides training and monitors the program jointly.

All these contributors are made in partnership by different stakeholders as an ECD movement. There are more and more communities expressing the desire to establish the centres. By the year 2004, there will be atleast 25 centres established in this village, enabling about 700 rural children to enjoy their development rights.

The training is usually of 15 days and is residential. The basic training curriculum includes creative a play environment for the holistic development of children. Health, hygiene, sanitation, nutrition is an important part of training curriculum. Producing low cost materials from the locally available resource is another important aspect of the training. At the initial stage the trainees learn the facilitators of the centre learn to follow a semi structured day schedule. Later with experiences and improved skills, more flexibility is adopted. The training is not an easy one it has lots of challenges for the resource persons and the trainees both.

Changing weakness into strength

The participants usually bring their young children along with them as there is no one to take care of them at home. Since we cannot avoid this situation, the training team has to create an environment for these children as well. These children provide an opportunity to gain first hand experience for the participants.

The training is a turning point for many women for their own self development and for outside exposure, which also prepares them to take a leadership role in the community.

The newly trained facilitators also receive training on Parenting Education. Parenting education expands and strengthens their link with the parents whose children are attending ECD centre. If you are lucky you may come across a parents' group having a dialogue session with the facilitator and having reflection on the change they have seen in their children, at home as well as from the experiences in the centres. Parenting Education's goal is to meet the holistic development goal of ECD for the younger children at home situation, Increase knowledge, skills, confidence resulting in strengthened caregiving practices, Impact on 0-3 years as well as older children, Creating opportunity for parents to articulate while enabling children to function effectively in rapidly changing society, Developing parents' ability to articulate to local government/NGOs their support needs for their children.

ECD movement is not just a program for 3-5 year children. It is a set of programs comprising home based, entrypoint, ECD centre and older children's program too.

Home Based program is usually for 0-3 years old children. Household activities occuring in a family example, bathing, washing the dishes, preparing for cooking, cleaning the house, oil massage greatly influence a growing child's learning in a child friendly learning environment at the household level, within the framework of existing financial resources, time and manpower. Father's involvement in home based activities reduces the burden of work on women. The program also to aims to reduce gender discrimination at the family level. Home Based program activities provide children with opportunity for their multidimensional development.

There is another program that is taking place in the same village which is for children between 1 1/2 to 3 years. It is the seven mothers program. Each mother take care of children from seven families on a rotaional basis. Entry Point program is implemented in families/ communities where there is pressure of workload, time and poverty. It involves parents specially mothers forming themselves into groups. Fathers play an important supportive role. They develop play educational play materials from the locally available resources. Parenting Education is the key to building parents' awareness and move from awareness to action. From the Home Based program the children move to Entry Point program and then from the Entry Point program the children move to the ECD centres. From the ECD centre, the children are enrolled in the school. This the outcome of right based early childhood development program.

What happens when there is a continuous increase in numbers of these centres?
One centre among every ten will be identified as a model centre. The model centre room is usually about 25 x 35 feet. It definitely will need an outside financial support. The size of the room is not only to accomodate 25 children, but also to serve as a learning centre for the new facilitators. The model centre must have a well set-up program with child-centred activities, low cost and with high quality. Parents participation is a must. Model centre is to demonstrate a model program that can be replicated in the rural setting.

There will be atleast nine ECD centres around one model centre.

Facilitators of the other nine centre come together twice in a month to this model centre. District level Seto Gurans resource person makes it sure to participate in this one day workshop. New ideas and new theme is discussed in each workshop. New song and new rhyme is composed and practised, folk songs, dance, and traditional stories and games are given importance. Creative ideas are introduced. New story is developed. The group explores together what is new that is going on in their community – birth, marriage, naming day of a new born baby, or a festival? Is it a plantation time or harvesting time? Is it a spring season or a rainy season? Anything maybe a theme for learning.

A model centre is identified not only by the size of the room but by the perfomance and skills of the facilitator. She is the local resource person. A local trainer. Role of the model centre is crucial, specially at remote and rural areas, where experts seldom manage to reach and where monitoring is not regular and systematic. The facilitators gain confidence when they receive each others' support and not to feel isolated because of remoteness.

As you travel in this village, you will discover that Mechhe is the first village in Nepal where such a solar module is piloted. You may also ask how long has this been going on? All this has happened within a period of one year. It has taken a year's effort for community mobilization. Now each community has developed its own management committee and assigned to it the responsibilities to manage the centre smoothly.

The sustainability of the centre is another issue. Government pays nominal amount of salary to the facilitator. Community is usually poor and cannot collect enough money among themselves, to contribute a fair amount of salary to the facilitator who has to undertake such a big responsibility. The financial struggle is always there. Should the financial constraint deprive the children of their rights or how long will this poverty continue?
There are two strategies at peoples' choice. The Maoist principle and ECD principle. This implies to the government, whether to invest on weapons or invest on early childhood development.

We must prove that some day in near future, the cycle of poverty can be broken by the ECD movement by enabling the children of poorest of the poor, the capacity to think creatively to solve their own problem. Violence brings only destruction not development and peace. The government and the political parties all must compromise on the matter of early childhood development as the children's rights and the children are zone of peace.

After you come back from this trip you may wonder what difference this programs have made in the life of the children. Here are some of the key findings regarding the impact of participation in ECD programs on school enrollment, achievement and retention.

ECD Impact Study - Quantitative and Qualitative

Enrollment, achievement, retention, gender/ caste breakdowns (comparing children who have participated in ECD programs with those who have not)

Initial Enrollment into Grade 1

n   20% more ECD than non ECD children actually start school.

n   Difference in school starting rates are specially striking for girls and for children from disadvantaged groups.

From these findings we are assured that ECD program in child rights framework can make significant impact on children's development which is the foundation for social change in the communities of the poor.

The child is a nomad on the border with the present

Aldo Masullo

Aldo Masullo

University of Naples, Italy

I must confess that I had a very peculiar feeling whilst I was waiting for my turn to speak, due to the fact that here there are people who have already met several times and so there is a sort of great familiarity, whereas I am taking part in a meeting which has no precedent for me and so I am like a child meeting adults. I think that this could be an interesting topic, children and their extraneousness.

What characterises a child with regard to the adult is that where adults in general have common codes of communication, common complicities, fight but then come to an agreement, they also go to war in the stupidest way: all this is extraneous to children.

A child is not yet capable of understanding the meanings of the words that are pronounced by adults, the child is aware of the creeping complicity between adults that makes them all seem to be against him, the child is really a being like the famous E.T. in the film of the same name, he is lost in a place where he has never been before. I think that we ought to remember this experience that anyone can have in life when they enter a society where they have not taken part in its ceremonies and rituals, that anyone of us can have, for example, when we enter a room where a language we don't know is being spoken and there is this terrible and radical sensation of extraneousness. This must make us aware of the problem facing us when we talk about our relationship as individuals, as institutions and as a society, with children.

It is certainly remarkable that however many efforts have been made, especially in our culture, no-one has ever succeeded in clearly distinguishing, not even from the terminological point of view, at what age one is a "child". We call children those who in some ways are not even little boys or girls, who cannot speak yet, but we also call children those in the first stages of their speaking life and we even call young people children; in some classifications they are even as old as 18 or 19. Naturally this does not help us understand the multiplicity of the worlds we approach when we confront the problem of the child. Moreover the child does not exist as a category, children exist. Apart from the problem of different ages, there is not a single child that is the same as another one.

The child has the stigma of individuality. In front of a child we must realize that we do not have an example of a species in front of us, but a unique species, that particular child.

It is clear that this makes the problem of the relationship between the world of adults and the world of children extremely complex. The first thing that I would like to say is that the relationship with children is not a professional relationship like others, it is a vital relationship and our existence, the existence of each and every one of us, depends on it.

Now we have to tackle the problem of children, of how to approach children and how the institutions can be organized to approach children. This is more serious and harder than it seems, because if it is true that every child is an individual, then how can an institution, which in some way is an impersonal body, relate to such an exquisitely personal and individual entity as an individual child? This is the problem of schools, because here we are talking above all about schools. The problems that concern the child pertain certainly to all the social functions but school is the place par excellence of the encounter between the adult and child. "School" begins essentially with the first relationship between mother and child and all the subsequent relations are just as vitally essential relations as that of the mother or whoever replaces her, with the child when a newborn.

Regarding children's rights, I do not have any direct competence and therefore I can only accept the provocation when someone said: let's ask the philosopher.

I am always slightly worried when people say, turning to me, that they are talking to the philosopher. I am only a modest teacher of philosophy. In my time, the philosophers were called Plato, Aristotle…

However, I must confess that I am not only a modest teacher of philosophy, I am also a philosopher. Now of course you may be horrified: just now you said something very humble and now suddenly you are full of pride. There is no contradiction: because I am a philosopher and I say so for the simple reason that I am a person who is very concerned by his existence and who pays attention to his existence.

This means being a philosopher: being concerned about your existence.

It is clear that when you are concerned about your existence, it can safely be assumed that you are also concerned about the existence of others and in particular people whose natural fragility and as yet lack of determination can only make your own existence more meritorious.

In a certain sense, then, I would say that it is incorrect, or not logical to speak of the right of a child, in the sense that we know that rights are none other than social institutions and that rights derive from decisions and from conventions.

Now, when a child is born, he does not take part in the agreement on which civil society is founded. We, as heirs of the modern state, all know that rights are not given to us from above, from God, but are given to us by popular agreement, by the agreement of all; there is nobody's right that has not taken part in the institutive agreement of the right and the child has not taken part in that institutive agreement.

So we have to think of one basic thing, that child does not have a right, but with the child the root of all the possible foundations of rights comes into being.

When a child comes into the world, he cannot speak, he has no code and he would never become a human being, he would be an individual of a zoological species called homo sapiens, if the child were not, as a great German philosopher said, invited to communicate and to relate to others.

And the first person to invite him is his mother or whoever acts in her lieu, the first person to invite him is the person who, with a smile and a caress, asks the child to communicate; this is communication of bodies before communication of minds or before communication of spirit.

The child is that mode of human existence that indicates to us the root of that transition in which we live continuously, in the continuous passage between our natural genetic endowment and our participation in an infinite horizon of knowledge, ideals, intentions and fantasies.

Here we are at the root, and so rather than speaking of right, we ought to speak of child of the right, of the moment of birth, of the system of society, a moment that is expressed in relationships of needs and submission to the rule that every need entails.

This immediately highlights how the child is not only the first chapter but the capital chapter of all human life.

Naturally this means that competences, research factors and institutional organizations must be summoned and work together around the child. All this put together would not be sufficient if it were reduced to a pure and simple social construction with an impersonal character, if in this great skeleton of coordinated social functions, there were not the continual concern that each of us has for our own existence: being concerned with and understanding what existing means. We cannot educate and provide for children if we have forgotten about them.

It is a particularly important fact of human society that adults forget about themselves. Adults in the cultures of countries which are still on this side of major technological and economic development forget about them, as we have heard today from our friends to whom I express my admiration and my human solidarity.

But this poverty is also ours, we who live in a technologically advanced and economically developed society.

We identify ourselves in an enclosed place to listen, enclosed in the strain of listening. But I have now emerged from that mode, now I am not listening, I do not feel the responsibility to understand, I feel the responsibility of speaking and communicating.

This is existing. How many times do we forget about this small detail of our life and let ourselves be totally expropriated by ourselves, in the name of a pure principle of performance, which is a principle which has inspired all societies?

Each society has no other principle to impose other than that of performance, because every society wants its individuals to serve its interests of a formative nature.

The principle of performance counts, but when we approach man we want to try to make him really become what he has the right to become.

We are speaking about the right to become because a child, when it is born, is not yet a person, but has inside the conditions to become one. Preventing the child from becoming a person is the full sense, a person who autonomously governs his existence but is purely and simply submitted to the principle of performance, means denying the child the possibility of realizing that principle of the child's right, that principle of humanity without which the child remains a cog in the wheel, albeit very important, in a mechanism which may well be perfect but where he is the cog in the wheel and we, the society of adults, are the mechanism.

We have killed life, we have killed imagination and we have killed creativity. This is why I find the title of our conference very beautiful. I think that the first thing it bring to mind is that to be able to speak, even only amongst ourselves about children, we cannot shut ourselves up into the specializations of individual fields of knowledge: I am the psychologist, I am the philosopher, I am the cultural anthropologist, I am the pedagogue and so on.

The child as a human being who aims to mature the fullness of himself, is not made up of segments, just as a patient for the doctor is not made up of different segments, nor is the person you love made up of different segments.

This is an ethical fundamental principle before being a principle of a pedagogical and then ethical nature, and so we have to cross borders. There are no borders that can keep us in the territory and prevent us from going into the next one. We certainly have to do so with care, with respect and bearing in mind that every discipline has its mediations, its codes, every competence therefore is incompetence but not improvisation.

Competences can be maintained only if we have the courage to let them crossbreed with others.

And so the first phase is communication across borders. Today we can travel throughout the European Union without a passport, but there are still too many passports in our habits and in our culture. All passports should be abolished.

What is important is that we feel together our apprehension in understanding who that third party is, that it is neither he nor I and that it is the child.

I would like to pay a small and modest tribute to the "unknown child", unknown because every child is unknown and the child as such is unknown.

From many sides we try to penetrate him as if a fortress under siege, but we will never really be able to get inside him. We can only allow him to let us practise feeling increasingly together with him: this is a fundamental point.

Is school, real school, an activity of a professional nature on the teachers' side, or a need that is more or less laid down by law on the children's side who are obliged by their parents in the more fortunate countries to go to school?

School is essentially freedom, an exercise of life, but I can never really enter the soul even of the person I love, because each of us is unreachable in his individual essence. I can't even reach my own individual essence, so what can we do? By living, I can accentuate the tension of my life and feel the tension of other lives better. There is a very beautiful poem where, speaking of two people in love, it says that we are like two different violin strings but we practise on the same string of the instrument, and in this common exercise a single sound emerges but we remain two different people and do not merge but nevertheless the sound is the same.

I believe that this in some way is the paradigm of educating, the paradigm of our relationship with the child, this sort of continuous provocation, like the invitation I spoke about at the beginning. Each one invites the other, each one in some way seduces the other but not in the perverse sense of the word, in the sense that one attracts the other, invites him but without wanting him to lose his freedom.

And here we are at the antipodes of the principle of performance: a real school is the one that is not at the service of a society to make individuals the instruments of a principle of performance and collective interest, but a real school is the one where each person who operates in it, stimulates and invites each of the small young individuals to express their freedom: I believe that this is the great horizon of education.

We have to realize that school is not school in the ordinary sense of the word, it is not one of the many institutions, that teaching is not one of the many traditions, but that school, like teaching, is a place of myth, in the proper meaning of myth, something that never coincides with material reality but that represents our ideal of life, a myth of encounter.

If you think about it, you will realize that in all social activities there are always at least two sides that meet, whose interests are in contrast because the shopkeeper has to sell his worst product at the highest price and the customer has to buy the best product at the lowest price.

These interests are in contrast with one another and society is the place where these contrasting interests meet, collide, mediate and, through a little deception and fraud and a little acceptance of what suits us best, we end up by carrying on.

This happens everywhere, but in schools do those who teach and those who learn have two opposing interests or do they have the same interest?

Certainly, the objective interest of those who go to school as pupils is to learn, but the interest of those who teach is not to teach, the interest of those who teach is to learn as well.

I always say that I consider myself young despite my many decades, as long as I want to learn. School is the place where people of different generations have in common the desire to learn and the teacher is not someone who teaches but someone who learns as well but, because he has more experience, is able in some way, to help and guide others to seek that truth that has many facets and is never identified as truth with a capital T but represents the basic principle of man, opposing the principle of performance, because whilst the principle of performance imposes on us to do everything that is useful for society even if false, the principle of truth is the principle to which our freedom takes us.

There is a beautiful passage in Immanuel Kant's Anthropology in which he says: have you ever wondered why all the great revolutions fail?

It is an extraordinary question. Kant asked this question at the end of the eighteenth century, in one of his later writings. He thought that even the French Revolution was fundamentally ending badly. All the great revolutions end badly, and yet they are revolutions which are often thought out. The principle of freedom and equality, the rights of man: what is more thought out coherently with humanity's need than these principles?

What was the October Revolution in Russia? The idea, in principle, of achieving real equality and consequently the real freedom that the French Revolution had been able to imagine but had not succeeded in creating.

And yet that one also failed, and it failed miserably. Why? asks Kant.

And Kant gives an answer: all the revolutions studied by wise men, perhaps around a table after having consulted entire libraries, are revolutions which are inevitably carried out by the generation that conceived them and this generation, however forward it may be in thought, remains backward in its nature, backward in its psychology and backward in its customs.

It was to be Freud that would understand this contrast very well between what is aware and what is inside us, is settled within us and makes us determined.

Imagine what there is between these two polarities: a generation that imagines innovation, has great thoughts but has fallacious actions. What lies in the middle? There is the need to bring out generations capable of understanding and continuing those great thoughts, but structurally, I would say almost physiologically trained in a new way: this is the great challenge.

Imagine what this challenge must be today in the 21st century, when as we have all acknowledged, all changes are taking place much faster than in the past. But these are purely mechanical, technological and material changes that end up by weighing on our daily lives and on our character whilst they should be liberating changes.

I think that here there is no other possibility, no other way out than that of understanding the decisive importance of young people.

A new education must be proposed for children. But if we are the ones who educate them and we are badly constructed and yet we have to try to have more rights asserted for them, what is the secret, what is the method?

There must not be the teacher and the pupil again between them and us, there must not be two dialoguing parties between us. We have to understand them as far as possible and make them able to understand us and what we are imagining as new and which we cannot make happen. This is why I increasingly insist on the need for dialogue between generations, because it is the most serious problem of society. A very strong example of this is that of having to be transformed and become new without interrupting one's relationship with the past.

At the beginning memory was talked about and it is a very good thing to recall memory but we must remember that memory can be only a stone monument that no longer says anything, except the fact that it occupies a certain space in the city and at a certain moment we look at it indifferently.

Memory is a tool, what is alive are memories, memories are always different and always new: what do I remember about the war?

Memory is written in books, there are those who write about it one way and those in another, I remember what I experienced of the war and I still feel those emotions inside me, but probably I already feel them differently from how I experienced them. This is the multiplicity of the conditions in which we live and therefore the enormous difficulty of relating to young people, to those who do not have great memories and on whom we think we can impose our legacies.

We have to try each time to live from scratch together with them and make new memories for them and make new memories for us: creating the solidarity of memories.

I believe that this is a fundamental point that is not only a point of an emotive and psychological nature: it is a point of social nature, it is a point of a collective nature and relates to the very destiny of humanity.

I want to underline that it is necessary to distinguish society from the community and please understand these two terms not according to the professional lexicon of philosophers, sociologists and psychologists, but trying to attribute to each of these two terms a concept that is unlikely to be asserted in traditional concepts or traditional terms.

Society, we have said, is the organization of individuals and society can only have one major aim which is to squeeze out the maximum performance from individuals who are part of it, to obtain the maximum results that are of interest to society (who programmes the interests of society and how is another matter which comes under another topic which we will leave aside).

Society is this mechanism, but the relationship between mother and child, that relationship without which the capacity to communicate is not created in the child, without which the capacity to use language is not created, without which the capacity to reason logically is not created (because logic is also a social function), this relationship between the mother and child, a relationship from which society is born, is it a relationship of a social nature or not?

If it were a relationship of a social nature we would find ourselves face to face with a contradiction, because if this is the relationship through which society is created, how can society come into being from a social relationship?

In that case the social relationship, society, would be established even before being established. It is once again the problem of the passage from nature to culture, the passage from before to after, from one sphere to another.

A child and mother do not have a common linguistic code. The child is all eyes, the child cries, the child seeks the mother's breast perhaps more for warmth than for food. The mother already has a language, but cannot use it with her child. And so what type of relationship is established? A child and mother form a community, not a society.

A community is the personal relationship between people, first at the base of every relationship and then with a social nature. Society is built up, the community lives together.

I would like to draw your attention to the relationship between the generation that teaches and the generation that learns at school: it is not a relationship of a social nature as in all the other functions of society but it is a common relationship.

School is therefore on the border, at the limit of society but not the limit where society ends but where society is born, where society is renewed and what is renewed humanly is not yet born.

At times we are dead and we do not realize it, if we have lost our ability to feel our existence and therefore to feel the existence of others and enter into a relationship which is emotional and intellectual at one and the same time.

This is another of the separations that we must overcome. We know nothing about the emotion of an animal so we cannot say what it really is. But real emotion is what comes at a time when feeling tired as perhaps I am feeling now, I also feel myself as someone who is becoming tired in order to communicate with others.

My emotivity is fuelled by intelligence, that is by an effort to understand myself and others and without this my personality would be pure and simple physiological movement. On the other hand, the same happens with reason or rational intelligence.

In general why are despotic dictators stupid?

This is a difficult question: they are stupid because, although they have a good IQ, they lack the warmth of the passion of a relationship with others, they lack the passion of their own existence, they are avaricious and they do not have a passion for existence.

And when we have extinguished the passion of existence in ourselves, we extinguish it in others as well, we create social and intellective monsters but we certainly do not contribute to life, to the renewal of society, we do not let communities be reborn.

There is a very beautiful proposition by Plato which says that small popular communities are so dangerous that tyrants hate them and are frightened of them.

This is because society, whether it is tyrannical or not, always requires principles of performance. Small groups made up at the same time of emotions and intelligence, are great popular revolutionary movements: this seems to me to be real problem of schools and therefore the centrality of schools.

Schopenhauer said that schools are necessary for the state because his idea of school is as a tool of the collectivity which proclaims the principle of performance. But the true, modern, new school cannot be inspired by the principle of performance; already the idea of democracy generally makes us think of a system of juridical organization of society, a system of juridical organization of the selection of power.

Democracy is certainly this as well, but democracy, before being a concept in itself or a system of organization of society, is a fundamental feeling; that feeling that, whoever I have in front of me, makes me aware of a feeling of fraternity: he is not like me because we are all different from one another, but although he is not like me, he belongs to my same brotherhood.

This is democracy. How many times is the jacket of democracy worn but inside there is the soul of someone who considers those who are different for any reason whatsoever with contempt?

Of democracy there is only the form, but if democracy is reduced to form, sooner or later it comes to an end. For a democracy to live, it has to be nourished by the life of feeling and intelligence, of feeling truly that we all take part in the same human destiny and therefore everyone is involved, responsible and summoned to be responsible not for the laws that always belong to the past - they are always before us - not for tradition that is always before us, but we are summoned to be responsible for our contemporaries, but above all for those who represent our future.

Responsibility means being summoned to answer those who will come after us, responsibility is feeling constrained to give an answer to whose who will come after us and whose lives will depend on the decision we take. This is the central point.

And so who is that child? The child is the one who is on the border, not between the past and the future, but the present. The child is a border subject, the child is a border nomad, he has not yet found his country and will never find it if he stays alive because the real country cannot be identified in any place in particular. The real country is our continuous anxiety of searching to give meaning to our existence.

And so school is really school only when children are educated and guided at the same time. Not to be subjected to habits, rules and discipline, but to organize their freedom, to conquer the freedom of themselves as a continuous need for search.

If all over the world we were spurred on by the same need to search for meaning, you can be sure that there would be no more war, there would be no more injustices by one people over another people, there would no longer be any tyranny, and we would all really be driven in the direction of this search for meaning. Reality and idealism, rationality and poetry would at last meet.

(not revised by the author)

crossing boundaries

attraversar confini

narrative on the possible
eleven concurrent sessions

The international conference 'Crossing borders'
(February 2004) contributed in a particularly effective way
to redefining cultural identity and politics
of the educational experience in Reggio Emilia.
It was an extremely privileged context within which
the different studies and research carried out
in kindergartens and nursery schools were summarised,
with glimpses also of elementary schools,
in relation to different interdisciplinary and multicultural approaches.
The dialogue sessions became locations and spaces for dialogue
among '100 languages, where didactics is interpreted
as a daily approach, as a metaphoric
and also realistic view of nursery school life,
and a place where theory and practice
re-produce and are reciprocally re-shaped.
They represented a chance to compare inter-disciplines
with interlocutors who are both inside and outside
our educational experience.
Voice was given to the schools/kindergartens, to the children,
to the teachers, to the parents, to the educating community,
to the city; where a variety of languages,
images, set-ups and sounds
were used to communicate...
• the theories of the sessions wanted to try
to clarify certain topics within each dialogue session:
how the research/exploration
into the history of the educational experience
in Reggio Emila is collocated,
to what other previous research
they make reference
• what efforts were made to update the languages
and to reread them in the light of the present day
• what questions, queries, doubts orientated
the focuses which were presented and discussed:
in an attempt to emphasise the more shadowed
aspects and the questions which still remain unanswered
 or those still to come.
• what sensitivity and advantages have emerged, useful
also to re-interpret daily actions
and implement a didactic idea as a place for comparison:
a didactics which is capable of restoring visibility and legitimacy
to the potentialities expressed by children
(the culture expressed by infants,
schools as places where culture is produced...)

We became friends anyway...

Recognising the differences

The educational/rehabilitation project
For the child with special rights
Among special rights, among obligations and possibilities

We became
friends anyway...

Making learning visible
The language of evaluation

Poetry in the digital era
utopias, metaphors and prospects
for possible futures

The enchantment of writing

The difference in ethics or the ethics of difference?

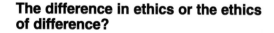

Democracy which participates in change
experiences of public and private cooperation

The unexpected cities
living the locations creatively

The rights on the environment: children, spaces, relations
pedagogy and architecture

The science of research, poetry and beauty

I linguaggi espressivi dei bambini, il linguaggio artistico di Alberto Burri

MUSEI CIVICI
16 Novembre - 8 Dicembre 2002

Children, art, artists

A difference in ethics or an ethic of differences?

Contributions by

ETTORE BORGHI
professor of philosophy, member of ISTORECO

KHALED CHAOUKI
president Young Italian Muslims

DANIELA CHIOFFI
teacher, Balducci preschool

ANDREA GINZBURG
professor political economy, Università degli studi di
Modena e Reggio Emilia

CLAUDIA MAIELLA
teacher, Pascoli elementary school

DEANNA MARGINI
pedagogista, Istituzione Scuole e Nidi d'infanzia

MAURIZIO MORI
professor of biothics, Università degli Studi di Torino

TULLIA MUSATTI
head researcher, Istituto di Scienze e Tecnologie della
Cognizione, CNR, President Gruppo Nazionale Nidi
Infanzia

TIZIANA PIZZI
teacher, Girotondo infant-toddler center/preschool

ALESSIO SURIAN
Coordinator of professional deverlopment initiatives
Centro Educazione alla Mondialità

Case theory

Different cultures have elaborated
during the course of history
different ethics that have
potential meeting points
but also reasons for conflict.
All cultures have always assigned
the duty of conveying
the principles and rules for behaviour to
the educational structures.
In the present day contexts of cohabitation,
with increasingly more differences,
the meeting with others (carriers
of knowledge, of ethics, of values not only different,
but also very distant)
requires and reconstitutes the values of laicism,
of pluralism, of dialogue
and of comparison.
The session wants to propose
a debate on the possibility
and the necessity today to build a plural
and pluralist thought, which is capable
of understanding differences
and is willing to put them into dialogue.
Starting from the idea
of a child which is sensitive
to the ethical dimension of relationships
and the definition of the educational context
as a place for debate and the construction of rules
and values which can be shared
by the different subjectivities and communities.

Recognizing ourselves as different

The educational/rehabilitative project of children with special rights between obligations and possibilities

Contributions by

CAROLINA CANTARELLI
teacher, Tondelli preschool

ANNA MARIA DALLA VECCHIA
children's neuropsychiatric, Children's Neuro-psychiatry Department, AUSL - Reggio Emilia

VALERIA FERRETTI
teacher, Ariosto elementary school

RAFFAELE IOSA
technical executive regional school office for Emilia-Romagna, Ministry of Education

IVANA REGHIZZI
teacher, Balducci preschool

IVANA SONCINI
psychologist, Istituzione Scuole e Nidi d'infanzia

VALERIA UGAZIO
professor of Clinical Psychology, Università degli Studi di Bergamo, Scientific Director EIST

CARLO VASCONI
parent, president of FACE (family association of encephalopathics) Reggio Emilia

We becam friends anyway...

Case theory

The session is based on an intent
and a declaration that concentrate
on giving children,
none excluded,
the potential and the right to be accepted
with their individual "special"
differences.
This approach is necessarily based
on the knowledge of the identity of the child
with special rights that can emerge,
not only during the diagnosis, but also
in the interaction between
all the systems and subjects involved.
What has been gained by this
and can it produce the pooling
of a series of knowledge
in pedagogic practice?
The main point to consider
is the quality of the educational contexts
that can lead to the research
and development of the possibilities
and resources of a child
with special rights.
The session will attempt,
with its theoretical reflections
and visual documentations,
to emphasise the contexts that make
the learning processes of children
more approachable and interpretable
and a more conscious view
of the knowledge of adults.

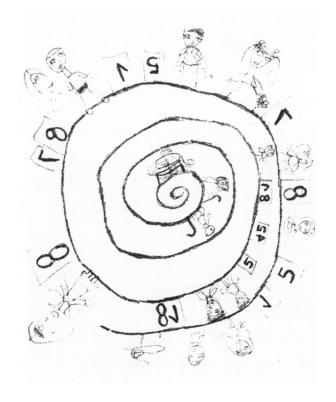

Children, art, artists

Contributions by

FLAVIA BARBARO
head of educational service GAM an museum Foundation Torino

PIER GIOVANNI CASTAGNOLI
director of the civic gallery of modern and contemporary art Torino

LUCIA COLLA
teacher, Bellelli infant-toddler center

FRANCO GUERZONI
painter

DJANET TAYLOR DESTAILLEURS
Projects Manager, project coordinator DAEP Centre Georges Pompidou, Parigi, Francia

ALFREDO HOUYELOS
doctor in Educational Sciences Pamplona infant-toddler centers, Spain

NORINA MARCELLO
head of neurology department, Hospital S. Maria Nuova, Reggio Emilia

LORELLA PRANDI
teacher, Bergonzi elementary school

BARBARA QUINTI
atelierista, La Villetta Villetta school

LORELLA TRANCOSSI
pedagogista, head of education and culture department, Comune di Sant'Ilario (R.E.)

VEA VECCHI
atelierista and collaborator Reggio Children

Case theory

We believe that poetic languages
are those which are most capable
of firmly holding together rationality,
imagination, sensitivity,
 and can become some
of the most effective antibodies
against violence and the most
productive vectors to listen
to others and other worlds.
The day is organised in different phases.
The theories are presented on the relationship
between children, art, and artists.
Using a series of visual testimonies,
we will be looking
at ateliers in schools and in museums
as places to promote
competent sensitive relationships
between children/youths and the artistic world,
making sure that the child is left
to be his own protagonist
of strategies and imagination.
An atelier within the school curriculum,
not relegated to marginal or optional roles
as so commonly proposed,
but as co-protagonists of the processes
of thought and knowledge
and as one of the 'guarantors'
of the connections and hybridisations
of languages.
The theory of the senses
as processors of knowledge and emotions
will also be faced.

The poetics of the digital

utopias, metaphors and perspectives
for possible futures

Contributions by

LANFRANCO BASSI
atelierista, Freire preschool

PAOLA CAGLIARI
pedagogical coordinator, Istituzione, Istituzione
Scuole e Nidi d'infanzia

CARMELO DI BARTOLO
designer, and director of Design Innovation, associate
professor University of Montreal, Canada

SUSANNA MANTOVANI
Dean of primary educational science department,
Università di Milano Bicocca

ROBERTO MONTANARI
expert in Human-Machine Interacion, Faculty of
Engineering, Università Modena e Reggio Emilia

GIOVANNI PIAZZA
atelierista, La Villetta preschool

TELMO PIEVANI
professor of genetic epistemology, Università di
Milano Bicocca

GRAZIA RICCI
teacher, Istituto comprensivo Lepido, European
project E3

MAURA ROVACCHI
atelierista, 8 Marzo preschool

DILETTA TIRELLI
teacher, La Villetta preschool

Case theory

The development of digital technologies
and telematic networks
is producing a remarkable change
in the methods of learning,
 of communicating, of build knowledge
and identities.
Schools generally tend
to confine technologies to computers
in specialised laboratories,
to chiefly teach computer science
and to separate technology and the sense of humanity.
The dialogue session will reason,
with trans-disciplinary contributions,
on didactic experiences
to prefigure contexts
of greater solidarity on what appears today
to be contrasted, and to build up
different cultural approaches
in school and in society.

Rights to environment: children, spaces and relations
pedagogy and architecture

Interventi

Rossana Barazzoni
teacher, Rodari infant-toddler center

Giulio Ceppi
architect and designer, TOTAL TOOL, Politecnico di Milano, Domus Academy

Antonella Davoli
teacher, Michelangelo preschool

Aldo Fortunati
Director of Istituto degli Innocenti di Firenze, vice-president Gruppo Nazionale Nidi Infanzia

Lella Gandini
University of Massachusetts, Amherst and US Liaison for the dissemination of the Reggio Approach

Elena Giacopini
pedagogical coordinator, Istituzione Scuole e Nidi d'infanzia

Michele Zini
architect and designer, ZPZ Partners, Politecnico di Milano, Domus Academy

Case theory

The planning of the infantile environment
is a fundamental element
in the construction of the identity
of a child, of a person
and in the self-learning process in every person.
The educational environment is structured
as a language that weaves the knowledge
and the semantics of pedagogy
with the knowledge and the semantics of architecture
and design together with the European standards.
The focal thread of this interlacement
can be seen in the attitude towards
research and in the attention paid
to the cognitive processes by children and teachers.
An unpublished and inexhaustible dialogue
emerges which is a transforming and poly-sensorial
dialogue
among spaces, materials, sensorial qualities,
documentation, children, teachers,
parents, pedagogists
and architects. In the dialogue session,
through the presentation of trans-disciplinary research,
an evaluation will be made on the idea
of rights to the environment as a right
to learn, acting and reflecting,
as a right, to take the time to understand
and to construct personal and group competences
and memories.

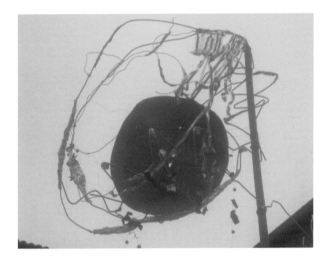

Sciences among research, poetry and beauty

Contributions by

M. GIUSEPPINA BARTOLINI BUSSI
Professor complementary di Mathematics, Università degli Studi di Modena e Reggio Emilia

RAFFAELLA BONETTI
teacher, nido d'infanzia Bellelli infant-toddler center

LUISA COSTI
teacher, Rodari infant-toddler center

ANTONELLO LA VERGATA
professor of History of philosophy, Università degli Studi di Modena e Reggio Emilia

PIERGIORGIO ODIFREDDI
professor of Logic, Università di Torino e Cornell, USA

PAOLA STROZZI
teacher, Diana preschool

STEFANO STURLONI
atelierista, Allende preschool

MADDALENA TEDESCHI
pedagogista, Istituzione Scuole e Nidi d'infanzia

Case theory

Sciences are fascinating due to their ability
to narrate the world but,
at the same time, they are intimidating
due to their transformation power
and their peculiar specificity
of languages.
It also seems that all sciences
are conceived from a common denominator
that also belongs to children
from when they are very young:
the amazement when faced
with the unknown and the tenacious desire
to ask questions and to look for solutions.
In the dialogue session
a variety of theories will be faced
including research as strategy
of knowledge,
emotion as an indispensable component
of scientific thought, poetry
as a possible form
of "scientific interpretation"
of reality and beauty as
an element of evaluation
of the elaborated theories.
These theories, proposed and sustained
by didactic experiences carried out
in kindergartens and nursery schools,
intend to promote
a reflexive and critical exploration
between the speakers
and the participants at the session.

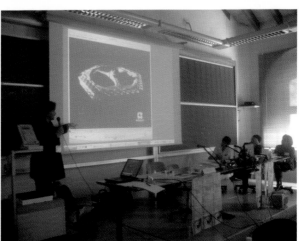

Making learning visible

The language of evaluation and assessment

Contributions by

PAOLA BARCHI
teacher, La Villetta preschool

GUNILLA DAHLBERG
professor of education, Institute of pedagogy
Stockholm, Sweden

LUCIO GUASTI
Università Cattolica di Milano, Board Member
Istituzione Scuole e Nidi d'Infanzia

MARA KRECHEVSKY
researcher, Harvard University Project Zero, USA

GIORDANA RABITTI
president of Reggio Children

CARLA RINALDI
pedagogista, pedagogical consultant to
Reggio Children, Università degli Studi di Modena e
Reggio Emilia

LAURA RUBIZZI
teacher, Diana preschool

STEVE SEIDEL
director, Harvard University Project Zero, USA

Case theory

Educational documentation -
a current theory present in many
national and international
pedagogic reports - finds an original
interpretation in Reggio Emilia
that places it within the didactic project,
that is during the entire course,
to direct it and improve the relations
of the disciplinary and cognitive structures
in children.
It is prefigured therefore
as an instrument which is capable
of modifying didactics
but also the individual and group cognitive processes
in children and adults.
The documentation, conceived in this manner,
also reveals itself
as a possible instrument for evaluation
and self-evaluation.
These theories will be presented
and discussed
with the participating public.

Town *in*waiting

creatively inhabiting the places

Contributions by

ANDREA BRANZI
architect and designer, associate professor at the Faculty of Industrial Design, Politecnico di Milano

MARA DAVOLI
atelierista, Neruda preschool

TIZIANA FILIPPINI
pedagogical coordinator, Istituzione Scuole e Nidi d'infanzia

ANNALIA GALARDINI
executive Educational Services Comune di Pistoia

AMELIA GAMBETTI
coordinator of Reggio Children, board member Istituzione Scuole e nidi d'infanzia

LORENA LUCENTI
teacher, Panda infant-toddler center

EVELINA REVERBERI
teacher, Diana preschool

MIRELLA RUOZZI
atelierista, Laboratorio G. Rodari

DENIS SANTACHIARA
designer

MILENA ZANTI
teacher, Balducci preschool

Case theory

Giving visibility to infancy,
its culture, its competences,
promoting the rights of children
to live from the very beginning
the cultural, political, and institutional locations
in the city, to sustain the strong liaison
between the destiny of children and adults
is what has characterised the dialogue,
the mutual listening,
the cultural and political interlacements
between the city of Reggio Emilia and its schools.
A school and a city, that give credit
to infancy and recognise its rights,
create fundamental grounds
for a true right of citizenship
and an active interpretation
by all those involved in the debate
on the 'problems of the city.
The session introduces therefore
the theories on the identity
of cities, on the models of habitability,
of the sense of affiliation and citizenship today,
proposing the idea of children as co-authors
with the adults of the research
on sense around the places of life.
With the presentation of the Unexpected City project,
which takes ideas from the re-reading of 'Grammar of
imagination'
by Gianni Rodari,
a children's view is proposed,
on certain places in the city,
which are funny, ironic,
unexpected, and capable of producing
new identities in places everyone knows
and, therefore, surprise our manner
of observance.

Music of the body

Contributions by

MAURO BIGONZETTI
artistic director Aterballetto

ADRIEN BOISSONNET
choreographer and dancer Aterballetto

DANIELA BONACINI
teacher, Peter Pan infant-toddler center

PAOLA CAVAZZONI
pedagogista, Istituzione Scuole e Nidi d'infanzia

DANIELA LANZI
pedagogista, Istituzione Scuole e Nidi d'infanzia

VALERIO LONGO
choreographer and dancer Aterballetto

BEATRICE MILLE
choreographer and dancer Aterballetto

PAOLA NOTOLINI
teacher, Robinson preschool

ALBERTO OLIVERIO
professor of psyco-biology, Università La Sapienza,
Roma

FEDERICA PARRETTI
choreographer and dancer

BARBARA PINI
atelierista, Choreia preschool-infant-toddler center

VIRGINIE RETORNAZ
Head National Center Childhood, Art, Languages,
Ville de Lyon, France

Case theory

The dialogue session intends
to reason and implement
the suggestive relationship between
body language
and the expressive potentialities
that are recognised to children.
The theory of the session
can be summarised in this declaration:
from **the body and the mind**,
to **the body is the mind**.
Therefore the communications,
the experiences, the narrations
that are introduced are offered
as ideas for a dialogue
and a debate around the idea
of a body which is inseparable from the mind,
a body impregnated with culture,
a multimedia body, expressive,
excited and exciting.
A body not only seen
as being anatomical and functional,
but as a carrier of different knowledge
and capable of constructing learning.
The identity and the contents of the session
indicate the relationship
between pedagogy and the different cultural
and scientific knowledge,
in particular the contributions
of neuroscience and the artistic world
of dancing.

The magic of writing

Between signs and writing.
How children approach written codes

Contributions by

Simona Bonilauri
pedagogista, Istituzione Scuole e Nidi d'infanzia

Giuliana Campani
teacher, Arcobaleno infant-toddler center

Roberta Cardarello
professor of General Didactic, Università degli Studi
di Modena e Reggio Emilia

Antonia Ferrari
teacher, Neruda preschool

Giacomo Stella
professor of Clinical Infant Psycology, Università
degli Studi di Urbino

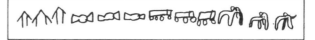

Children and figurative writing

Contributions by

ROBERTA CARDARELLO
professor of General Didactic, Università degli Studi di Modena e Reggio Emilia

CLAUDIA GIUDICI
pedagogista, Istituzione Scuole e Nidi d'infanzia

MASSIMO PITIS
graphic designer, BEDA (Bureau of European Designers Association, Barcellona)
Politecnico di Milano - Facoltà del Design

MARIAROSARIA PRANZITELLI
teacher, Calvino Elementary School

IRIDE SASSI
atelierista, Andersen preschool

Case theory

Children very precociously
and intensely encounter
the written codes
that culture, has given itself today.
From when children are very small
they elaborate theories
on the written code;
they pass through the construction
of personalised "codes" of communication
that, if adequately activated, become essential
for the construction of conventionality.
The learning of alphabetical writing,
as every other learning,
is a creative process,
that also implicates specific
and transversal competences
with other languages or areas
of discipline,
a learning that begins before
formalised teaching is introduced.
The session intends
to propose for discussion
the documentation of some coding
and decoding processes
used by children and
the importance
of activating generative contexts
in educational circles.
The project on 'figured writing'
will also highlight the relationship
between writing and language
and will be an opportunity
to reflect and to reconsider
written and spoken words,
the communicative expressiveness
of written text,
the relationship
between writing and images,
the communicative and metaphoric
potentialities of graphic language.

Participated democracy during change

experience of cooperation between public and private system

Contributions by

IRENE BALAGUER
pedagogista, Barcelona, Spain

SABRINA BONACCINI
pedagogista, Coordinator Divisione Infanzia
Coopselios

LORENZO CAMPIONI
executive educational services and school policies,
Regione Emilia Romagna

CRISTINA FUNICELLA
parent, Association Agorà

RACHELE FURFARO
Commissioner to Culture, Comune di Napoli

MIROSA MACCIÒ
Vice president Cooperative Totem

ALBERTINA MANOTTI
parent

LUISA MERLI
president Cooperative Panta Rei

PETER MOSS
professor of early childhood education Institute of
Pedagogy, University of London, UK

REBECCA NEW
professor Tufts University, USA

ALESSANDRO OVI
Director of Technology Review (Mit)

JUNA SASSI
Commissioner to education and culture, Comune di
Reggio Emilia

MARIANNINA SCIOTTI
Regional president FISM

SERGIO SPAGGIARI
director Istituzione scuole e Nidi d'Infanzia

TIZIANA TONDELLI
Administrative executive Istituzione Nidi e Scuole
d'Infanzia

AGATA THAPA
Seto Gurans National Child Development Services,
Nepal

Case theory

The challenge of education requires
considerable receptiveness
in order to interpret the social
and cultural changes
and translate them
into projects and innovation.
To correspond to the right
of citizenship and the right to education
of children today means
pooling all the resources
available on the territory,
both public and private,
to plan an educational system
for the community that is built
on negotiated rules and values.
The participation of parents,
of the public and private representatives,
of the associations,
of the administrators, and the technicians,
in this project is a democratic space
that valorises knowledge
and experiences in a dialogue,
which contributes
to consolidating a social bond.

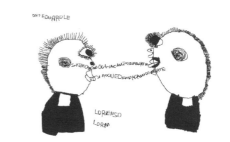

crossing boundaries

attraversar confini

Dedicated to Loris Malaguzzi

"Who am I?..."

Loris Malaguzzi

We are working in such difficult and changing times for a child driven beyond a capacity to foresee because the future today is difficult to govern.

I believe that the problem of children today is a major problem that requires a great capacity of selection, of making choices, choices that break away from the recent past and even the more distant past and that has in it at least the terms of a possibility, the terms of a possible trajectory that is capable of foreseeing, feeling everything that the present gives us today. In the present there are many things and many complex things, many intersecting things, many good things, many things that are not good, many bad things, there are many fortunes, many possibilities, many positive things and many risks... and I believe that our season is an extremely rich season of compositions mixed with the possibilities of extremely complex destiny.

I think that perhaps we could take as a start this sort of invocation by Alice which seems to me to be an invocation which can very well, and not only symbolically, be included in a sort of appeal to which we cannot be insensitive.

At a certain point, Alice, that extraordinary child (with a philosophy which is not only adult, but with an extremely rich juvenile philosophy that is extremely provocative) wonders in a soliloquy:

"Who am I? Tell me that first, and then, if I like being that person, I'll come up: if not, I'll stay down here till I'm somebody else. I do which they would put their heads down! I am so very tired of being all alone here."

I would say that very significant images are echoed here and I still believe that children today are asking us what they are.

The main question is absolutely not to stop children talking about themselves.

These are not simple statements because it is clear that there is an upheaval and that what has to be done is give them the ability, but how can you give them the ability if they are not granted the right? The right, that is, of being able to talk about themselves, or being protagonists identified in an identity that they like as well.

I think that taking this as a starting point (...) we could try to make an attempt at reconnecting the great designs, the great theories and the great problems that are linked with our everyday experience with children. It seems to me that Italian pedagogy is lacking this, shut up as it is in its books, in its writings, closed up in basements and attics, etc... in a continual and obsessive rereading of old writings about old inabilities and above all about absolutely confined and unliveable spaces.

I think that the first question is that there is a crisis, or the end, as I believe, of science as a teleological reference and rigid source, that knows everything and foresees everything. Try and infer something from this! It is the type of pedagogy that we can use where pedagogy appears as a science, but in one way or another some suspicions have to be raised. The indications that can follow are many, I believe that each of you can already find them in some way.

No knowledge expects to fill every possibility any more and the unforeseeable today is a category of science. This statement is connected with the first one but gives even more strength to the possible ways in which we can each interpret it.

Physics, chemistry, cosmology, cognitivity, neuroscience and cybernetics are rediscovering for the first time, and this is the fact that cannot be sufficiently repeated, their nature. This means that physics, chemistry, biology etc...which in some way have gone into hibernation through the rigid laws of science, are paying a heavy price and above all they are producing something of great value which is that of a necessary recombination of disciplines as each one not only understands that it cannot succeed, but understands what solidarity and a transcultural approach mean.

(...) On the pedagogical level, the Indications are also very clear, this slidarity, this interaction and inter-relation between the disciplinary forms, between the forms of knowledge, all this I believe we should try to review within our experience.

This means that we must have a less disjointed thought than we have been capable of to date and today we still proceed along a path of this kind, there is no time to talk to you about how disjunction, opposition and antinomy is a category that is widely used by the old type of science and because of the force and pressure of the old type of science – and you must not think that these are terms of a scientific nature only, they are terms of an economic order, of a political order and of an ideological order, this is the main question.

We have to try and produce maximum cognitive flexibility in ourselves but also in children.

Feeling that we are always ready to pack our bags.

Thinking of interconnecting, which is the great verb, I think, of the present and of the future, a great verb that we have to be able to understand completely and to decline it in all our efforts; bearing in mind that we live in a world which is no longer made up of islands but a world made up of a network... but in this image there is also the construction of a child's thought and our construction of thought, a construction that can no longer be made up of islands, which are separate but belong to a great archipelago and to a great network where interference, interaction and interdependence are the constant, even when we do not see them, even when we think that they do not exist and they are not there, there is interdependence.

Great attention to values, values are a fact of primary importance, I would say, and every selection and every choice and every ability to penetrate further into the great forest of the major issues of today - I believe however that the capacity of observation of the values that are values of a human order, ethical values, values of solidarity, of interdependence, values of capable organization finalized to ... rather than to... - these are the great values on which we have to work and these are also the great values which have to be in some way germinated in children.

None of us wishes to ban transmission, but there is transmission of a conservative nature and there is transmission of an innovative nature. The transmission of an innovative nature is that which not only takes us alongside the major issues, which we have tried to illustrate here, but it is the only way that truly allows us to produce a real and genuine approach to the child because the child's wish is precisely this, to be changed in an innovation which he feels as if it were a sort of physical sensation, of movement, of dynamics, etc. inside.

What can I say.. that on this image of the child and on this image of the right of the child to be seen, imagined, thought and above all experienced in these terms, there is a force that has in it the force of unhinging everything that surrounds it with meaning and essence, teacher training, the equipment needed, the significance and the identity of nursery schools in Italy.

In essence then, I would like to say that this figure of Alice asking to be able to come out is also the figure of every mother but it is also the figure of every father and it is the figure of every teacher and it is my figure, I mean it is the figure of everyone.

The child needs to produce situations of bewilderment, probably, in order to some way lower the threshold of routine which he is induced to experience both in the context of the family and of school.

...and I would say that his running towards us becomes a part of our running towards him... and it is perhaps in the happiness of this encounter that we can find the maximum mutual interpenetration, the maximum joint participation and the maximum oneness.

We have relied on this large figure, on this important figure.. and we receive some confirmation when we go around the world and hear that the same feeling can be found in all cultures. In all cultures you find great nostalgia for what is lacking for childhood and... you feel that alongside that consideration there is your own personal consideration, you who professionally and out of choice are an educationalist, being with children...you realize that you too are a victim, and not a secondary one, of the reduced prestige of children, of this childhood which is worth little.

...the child's intelligence is still today something in which we have to believe, we have to believe that the child is a bearer and constructor of his own intelligence. If we are ready to accept this, then we will modify many of our relations with him, many of our languages, and school will also in some way adapt to a child who is a constant provider of tests, requests and intelligent research.
I would also say that this anxiety or this passion for searching, in some way, clearly mobilizes everything, the whole person, the whole child. The child is a born researcher... I would say that his and our searching together for things that we do not know, searching for things that can improve our relations... all this in some way not only produces a marvellous understanding between the adult and the child, but I believe it forms the directional axis where intelligence is fuelled and I would go so far as to say it increases his expansive capacity to relate with things or between things and therefore it also produces a capacity of interaction, dialogue, enquiry, searching for things and relations between things and events, which to me seems to be in essence the massive force of what we call intelligence...

Another strong consideration is that we are living in a period which, beyond the presumed recognition of childhood, is offering us a series of images of children impoverished of their effective capacities, possibilities and resources; we are living in a time when other images appear which are more dangerous, where alongside a fragile, delicate, impotent and passive image of the child, one has been added of a child living in a perennial state of suffering. It is indeed through suffering that he grows and through suffering he learns and gets to know and so on.... an ordeal, as though it were something inevitable for children.
Our answer is an answer that is absolutely opposed to this, it is a very optimistic answer. We know very well what the limits of optimism are but also what optimism can contain. We are in favour of an image of a child who is extremely open, fully equipped from birth, full of resources, of capacities and of qualities. I would say that there is probably a need to define democracy differently, giving central importance to the subject and that is, to the capacity and will of individuals to act and above all to be recognized as free and responsible players.

Selection of videorecordings from the archives of the Centre of documentation and educational research of the Nursery Schools and Crèches Institution of Reggio Emilia
Edited by Marina Castagnetti and Vea Vecchi

Intelligence and determination to build up schools of quality

Tullia Musatti

Tullia Musatti
President of Gruppo Nazionale Nidi Infanzia

For me it is an honour and a pleasure to bring you the greetings of the association I represent, the National Infant-toddler Group. As many of you are not Italian and come from far away, I would like to present our association. Its members are nursery and pre-school teachers, educational coordinators, researchers and university lecturers who work all over Italy. The association was founded in 1980 by Loris Malaguzzi, who was its Chairman until ten years ago, and by some of us who are here today. Its aim is to offer opportunities to meet and discuss the life and social conditions of small children, the meaning of care and education in early childhood, the quality of schools and services for infancy and their prospects.

Our association's first meeting was held here in Reggio Emilia on the initiative of Loris and I am very moved to recall the contradictory feelings but also his courage in launching into this initiative. It was by no means out of a desire for further adventures that his long professional experience had already offered him nor out of a need for more cultural stimuli that his work with schools in Reggio already gave him in ample supply. No, what drove him was recognising that the very wealth of the cultural and pedagogical experience of various towns in nursery schools and pre-schooling needed to be reinforced in measuring up to one another, no longer relying solely on the sporadic opportunities that had always gone hand in hand with this experience, for which Malaguzzi's work had always been a point of reference. There was the need to build up a structure that could materialise this need for networking and that could allow a more systematic confrontation on the processes, ways and aims of this new way of educating infants. In other words, there was the need to create a new culture of infancy and Loris knew only too well that culture comes from the participation of a plurality of different kinds of experience and the confrontation between and through differences. This is why Malaguzzi did not shy away from the request "Loris, we have to build up a network and you're the one that has to take the initiative", and allowed many of us to mature together with the fantastic experience of nursery schools and pre-schools in many of our towns and cities. This is an enormous debt of personal and collective gratitude that the premature loss of Loris has by no means exhausted and, on the contrary, is an important legacy for us.

Over the years, our association, although small, has become an important point of reference for the political and cultural debate on early education in Italy.

I would like to underline that I consider it very important not only to characterise our association and our meeting with the friends of Reggio on this occasion too, but also to describe the fundamental elements of the best examples of experience with infants in Italy. Although this experience is based on educational practices and inspired by a philosophy which in many ways is similar, what these cases have in common is certainly not the acquisition of a pedagogical method but that they are all in the same culture, there is a way of approaching the analysis of the condition of children in our society, a common perspective of the different agents and agencies, family, education departments and local communities, local authorities and the whole of the city with regard to infancy, a common vision on the possibility that the services and schools for infants can represent a place of renewal and social participation in the city.

This perspective becomes tangible in some key concepts that I would like to briefly recall here because they are full of important consequences at this particular political and social time for our country and, in many aspects, the whole world.

The first key idea is that educating is not limited to offering children important social and cognitive experiences. It means acting so that children can have an important daily experience with other people who are highly significant for them from the social and cognitive point of view and that can form a memory and permanent trace of a social life of quality as a reference and support in their future life.

Building up this experience for children means implementing scenarios and educational processes that have been expertly conceived, with the cooperation of different players, with skills in different disciplines and with different professional knowledge, that of the teacher, the pedagogical coordinator and the researcher. These skills and knowledge must be interwoven in a rigorous and continuous reflection and shared in order to analyse the encounter between the intelligent identity of each child and the environment of life and experience offered to him/her.

But above all, to build up the experience of children and to make it truly significant, the contribution and cooperation of many people is necessary, from the group of teachers and all the school staff, to the parents and other members of the family, the administrative authorities and the political decision-makers.

These are the strong ideas behind our perspective. The idea that education is the product of an entire educating community in which different agencies and players, each with their own role, functional responsibilities, that the quality of education is not separable from the quality of the relations between the different members of the educating community and that to reach results of a good level everybody involved must make an appropriate commitment to the final aim.

Beyond the praise for the high level of results produced, I feel that I can state that it is above all this that we can read with pride, admiration and a sense of common feeling in the reality of the educating city of Reggio Emilia: this choral rigorous and constant commitment, shared by all, in giving all children an education of quality.

Our association, the National Infant-toddler Group, has always acted keeping an eye on the multiple scenarios that form the background to infant education: political scenarios(the decisions of the national and local governments; requests of trade unions), the scenarios of social transformation (changes in the family and in the place of children in the family and society), the scenarios of the ideal perspective on children's rights and needs, in the awareness that quality education depends on the quality of those choices and conditions and has to meet those perspectives. However, it is also in the conviction that conversely, educational services for early childhood are today fundamental places of the social quality of life in our towns and cities. They are also places of social encounter in the strictest meaning of the word: between children, for whom they often represent the only opportunity to experience positive sociality amongst peers, to feel good together today which includes the pleasure and strategies for feeling good together in the future. They are also places of social encounter between parents who can get to know other ways of taking their responsibilities for their children on equal terms and receive the support that comes from confrontation. This is a controversial issue in the agenda of much thought on the condition of parents today, that of the function that educational services can have as a place of support for the educational role of the parents. More than thirty years ago, Loris Malaguzzi said (concluding a conference in Reggio Emilia, in 1971): "We believe that it is right to provoke families to count for more in the education of their children". This is not the hypothesis of a school replacing families but the vision of school that supports them in their educational efforts.

Malaguzzi also insisted however on how services for infancy can represent a meeting place for families of different origin, culture or social class, who often live separate lives in our towns and cities but who discover one another through their common interest in their children, as active social subjects and as subjects with rights. This suggestion is truer and more important today than ever before, in Italy as in many other countries where different cultures meet and sometimes clash, and where often it is the children starting school that represents for many families the first encounter with a public social place, with a public institution in the most important meaning of the word.

Our schools are thus attributed with an important task not only as the fundamental places of the social quality of a town or country as a whole: not only because the same rights now and the same future rights have to be guaranteed, but because they have to be a place of social participation and where an exercise in democracy can be carried out.

TODAY. If we look around us in Italy today, and I apologise to our foreign colleagues, the panorama we see is by no means comforting. The national government is involved in reforming the educational system that questions many of the experiments of quality that have already been achieved and certainly precludes the path to their generalisation and future formulation. In primary schools, the organization of all-day school, which had successfully already taken on a broader educational vision for many years, is being attacked. For infants, there is the aim to redesign the places and ways they enter schooling according to the needs of the institution.

It is not only a question of cuts to the financial resources, but a conception of the social condition of infancy, the responsibilities of families and of the public idea, which goes in the opposite direction of everything that has been planned to date. A privatised management of children's lives is once again proposed, a low-profile interpretation is given to their rights, as social subjects once again reduced to consumers of present and future educational vouchers. No less serious, a very low profile is also given to their parents, who are on the one hand invited to go "education shopping" on behalf of their children, whilst on the other hand their real material and psychological needs in coping with their own responsibilities in the complex social and definitely not user-friendly organization of our towns and cities, are ignored.

If I recall the difficulties we are facing here, it is not just because we are in Italy and Reggio is an important piece of Italy, a reference and a banner for the battles in favour of the rights of children and their parents. I do so also because I know that at a different time and with different words these scenarios have been proposed or will be proposed in many other countries. And many of you have already had the experience of how difficult it is to fight a vision which ignores how the rights and well-being of many, the quality of our society, also depend on the way in which the rights and well-being of children are guaranteed inside our schools. This is why I do think it is worthwhile to say on this occasion too, just before we listen to, see and admire the experience of our friends in Reggio, that it is not about a miracle but it is an enormous and continuous investment of resources, intelligence and determination to build up schools of quality for all children. And that we necessarily have to make the same effort and investment, in other Italian towns and cities and in other countries to achieve the same results. And that perhaps knowing that there are a lot of us taking this difficult path can be of support and encouragement to us.

Education has many facets

Sergio Spaggiari

Schooling is going through a difficult time all over the world.

There are signs of contemporaneity that make us see that we are in the midst of a historic phase in which the value and importance of school education are questioned.

There are those who think, with a hint of irony and some truth, that "school is the longest, most boring and most expensive way to gain knowledge", others, a little more maliciously, say, "no…to become ignorant".

Many are investing so that schools are dematerialised and become a "click school" where interactions with a screen replace direct human relations.

In many countries, school is now conceived as a market asset that has to submit to the law of supply and demand and as such becomes a service on individual request and not a resource of the community.

There are those who are working so that schools retreat and withdraw into more reduced areas of intervention.

Moreover, it is before the eyes of all how the young generations are influenced, in the formation of their behaviour and knowledge, by other agents of formation: music, television, advertising, the cinema, the Internet and sport.

In short, school today seems to be losing meaning and its prestige.

At least where there are schools! Of course,

It is worthwhile remembering that for 120 million children in the world, schools do not exist and they have absolutely no right to education.

For many of these children there are more odious and brutal violations of human rights, such as sexual abuse, child-soldiers. child labour, the spread of AIDS and international trafficking in children.

These are atrocious violations.

We were all very disoriented by the news broadcast all over the world on 9th April 2003.

That day marked the fall of the regime of Saddam Hussein in Iraq.

That night in Baghdad, in the chaos of war, all the museums were looted of their archaeological treasures. On the same night in Baghdad, all the orphanages were emptied and in a few hours thousands of Iraqi orphans disappeared.

Sergio Spaggiari
Director of Istituzione Scuole e Nidi d'infanzia

Perhaps they ended up in international child trafficking. We do not want to forget these atrocities.

But we would like to remember how, of the many rights denied, the negation of the right to schooling can appear as the most insidious and common violence against children, as it represents a waste of the most extraordinary resource that we have at our disposal: human intelligence.

In synthesis, I could describe the historic reality that we are living through as a progressive approach to a deschooled world, a world without school, a world deprived of those places where people can be helped to grow and to learn, where each one can learn to think with their own mind and where a community can meet and enter into dialogue.

If the idea to empty and impoverish schools has so many supporters and so few opponents, then we can ask "what is the future for educating children and adults?" In a word, what are the prospects today for education?

Looking for a possible answer to this question is the reason for this Conference, a rendezvous that we have supported to reflect on three cultural theories that are strategic points of junction to reconsider education in the future.

1) To relaunch the issue of the rights and potential of children and adults to reassert what Loris Malaguzzi wrote "For some forty years, everyone who has studied children has ended up by discovering not so much their weaknesses and limits as the surprising and extraordinary strength of their potential and their talents."

We want to renew the value of this statement not only by exposing their negated potential or suppressed rights, but above all by giving concrete accounts of the "real and possible capacities" expressed by children in their processes of growing up and learning.

In a word, we want to bear witness to the fact that rights can become realities and that potential can be transformed into projects and proposals.

2) To give value to the first of the rights of every individual: the right to be the protagonist of their destiny, to build up their lives, to create their own identity and knowledge, in other words the right to learning understood as an individual right that requires participation, shared searching and the encounter with others, in the conviction that a person does not receive their identity and knowledge by mere transmission or simply accumulating facts or experiences, but acquires them through personal processes of formulation and construction, experienced and practised in social and environmental interaction.

Therefore identity and knowledge are the result of shared processes of learning, belong to the world of dialogues in encounters, of the contamination of ideas and interpersonal cooperation and are not nurtured only on self-reflection and introspection or transmission and one-way teaching.

3) The rediscovery of the strategic role of schools, not as a place where pre-established knowledge and values are consumed and received, but as a place of privilege where opportunities for research and reflection, dialogue and formulation, are produced, in other words where freedom, participation, creativity and critical thinking are exercised.

These three pedagogical theories, to be studied in greater depth and re-explored, can today bring ideas and experiences into dialogue to release hopes for a new culture of education.

It has been our wish to connote this hope with a metaphor that has given the title to this Conference: crossing borders.

I symbolically portray this metaphor as a character from mythology: Ulysses who, before the Pillars of Hercules, facing the infinity of the ocean, spurs on his companions to go where no man had every gone before, saying

"Ye were not form'd to live the life of brutes,

But virtue to pursue and knowledge high".

With this phrase, Ulysses invites his men to cross the insuperable limit of the known world to explore seas and territories never crossed before, starting off from the assumption that man is driven by a thirst for knowledge and the desire to seek out what is new.

Ulysses' invitation is our invitation to state that between possessing the truth and looking for the truth we prefer the latter choice.

"The ethical ideal is to remain within reasonable boundaries": with these words, Horace, the Latin poet, told us many centuries ago how important it was for human behaviour to have a concept of "boundary" as something that it was not good to cross.

Our civilisation is founded on this notion to a great extent.

Today, dominant culture is still obsessed by the concept of boundaries or borders (whether geographical, disciplinary. political, racial, religious ...).

The logic of this concept is clear and sound.

If a border is not respected, there can be no civilisation or culture.

I believe that the educational experience in Reggio, inspired by Loris Malaguzzi, has had the cultural courage to transgress this idea of "a boundary as a separating and insuperable barrier".

Loris Malaguzzi was a figure full of cultural restlessness which drove him to look for new questions and new answers to the interrogatives of life all the time, to cross the borders that separate places, ideas and disciplines, in other words to "jump over the wall" of the obvious, ordinary and irremovable, spurred on by a passionate desire to look for new paths to *go beyond* the horizons of old pedagogy and its theoretical and instrumental paraphernalia.

This is why Malaguzzi invited us to *jump over the wall*, because he was convinced that the more children's education began to be renewed the more it succeeded in crossing borders, transgressing conformism, breaching specialized closures and opening up to original and audacious scenarios.

In Reggio Emilia, the first convention to be broken came from the refusal of the image of the child consolidated in pedagogical and psychological literature: i.e. the refusal of an image made up of weakness, poverty and incapacity.

He tried to look at a child not only as the *recipient* of care but also as a *producer* of stories and relations: a child who from birth can read and actively and competently construct reality, an actor and protagonist of his/her own story, capable of interacting with adults and peers. as well as significantly influencing both.

This is a child with an enormous potential of energy which comes from the strength of those who want to grow and the richness of those who are curious and who can be surprised.

An idea of this kind coherently implies placing at the centre of educational attention not so much the problems of those who teach, of how and what is taught, but the *subjectivity of those who learn*.

This gives rise to an authentic and fundamental "cultural revolution".

If the child has theories, skills, questions and is the active protagonist of his/her own processes of growth, then the role of education undergoes a radical change, to appear not as a simple act of *transmitting* knowledge and skills, but as a complex *process* of self-*construction*. This is in full agreement with Jerome Bruner when he states that for children and adults knowledge is constructed and not received and meanings are created not offered.

This "cultural revolution" provokes extraordinary openings of opportunity to look for and build up a new pedagogy of infancy.

In short, it is a small-huge Copernican revolution, which has broken away from immobility, confinement and the stereotypes of the old school which, as Morin says, "teaches us unfortunately to isolate objects, to separate disciplines, disassociate problems and eliminate everything that brings disorder and contradiction".

In the next couple of days, with this Conference, we would like to pay tribute to this cultural revolution with a simple choice: letting teachers speak and, through them, the children and bringing to your attention projects and activities that can bear witness to the wealth of the gifts and capabilities of children.

It is difficult to let children speak.

It is not easy to restore children's real voice, without falling into falsification or distortions.

Often, in books, films and even conferences, the words that carry children's voices take on a strange softened flavour that makes them lose their freshness and authenticity.

Adults are not very used to listening and too often have remained deaf and insensitive to the words and thoughts of children.

Children have been talked about without listening to them at many, too many, Conferences.

In practice and without realizing it, silencing them.

Over the next few days, however, we would like to let them express their 100 languages and this is why we will make room for the stories and documentation that can give the right value to the leading roles of children and their teachers.

Therefore the eleven sessions of dialogue, the exhibitions and displays, the meetings in the nursery schools and pre-schools and the publications of Reggio Children aim to represent an unusual opportunity to introduce us to a "special world" which we have defined "Narrative of the possible".

The artist Paul Klee was fond of repeating that "Art must not produce what is already visible, but has to make visible what no-one can see yet". Education also has to fulfil that huge task: to make the invisible visible. Narrative of the possible, in its variegated forms and in its different proposals, thanks to the contribution of teachers and educationalists, aims to make visible the great hidden potential of children, showing us an extraordinarily rich and unexpected infancy that, perhaps many of us would be happy and proud to meet more often.

We have spent many years denouncing betrayed rights and wasted intelligence and today we feel the duty and we have found the courage to relate the potential expressed and the capabilities that are possible.

I want to be frank: I don't know whether the quality of the results will be equal to the seriousness of our intentions, but we felt we had to try.

To prove that another type of education is possible.

In a world where for children there only appear to be scenarios of suffering and violations, where for children we only get news of tragic events and difficult lives, we want to show that perhaps there is still room to expect something good and positive. We all want to meet people who can bring messages of hope and announce optimism.

As educators, we have the duty to cultivate the seed of trust and nurture the desire to get to know the "planet of infancy" better and learn more about it.

We know that we do not know enough about how children learn.

We still know too little about how a child learns, how knowledge and opinions are formed, how an idea takes shape and which and how many strategies are required for thought and language.

We are still too ignorant in this to be able to afford the luxury of not documenting and not doing research.

This is why I believe that the task of the educator is to listen, observe and document, trying to collect from the impalpable reality of children's lives the signs, the references, the connections that enable even the most obscure processes to be interpreted and evaluated.

Gustave Flaubert said of himself, in a not very poetic way: The writer is like a hydraulic pump, he has inside himself a pipe that reaches down into the guts of things, into the deepest layers. He sucks on it and brings up everything that was below the ground and that could not be seen".

The educator also has this function: to bring to the light the intricate adventure of human learning that is often implemented invisibly and to try to give shape and meaning to what was a simple gesture, look or sound.

In this sense the educator is a **researcher.**

I am against the idea that many academics have cultivated around the educator as a **carrier of raw material** (texts, stories, photos, videos) to deliver to scholars who then keep for themselves the role of reprocessing and researching the material.

No, educators are not to researchers as cotton-pickers are to fashion designers. No, educators are also fully entitled to be researchers.

It is possible. It is possible if we go beyond the known threshold of pedagogy.

Narrative of the possible helps us to look at original fields and horizons, where we can have the pleasure of discovering that monocultures and fundamentalisms can be overcome and that science can dance with art, music can dialogue with mathematics, imagination can gallop along with reason and with ethics, that poetry, computers and architecture are things that can get on together and that all this, extraordinarily, can happen at school, even in schools for the very youngest children.

It is my conviction that school today has to begin to understand that it is possible to change and improve the educational offer and to understand that education has many facets, not just one.

Education can be a factor of conservatism or of change, it can act to suffocate and subjugate or to emancipate and liberate, it can create conflict or social cohesion, it can be authoritarian, standardizing and monocultural or pluralist, understanding and exciting.

In short, education can be an exercise of freedom and practice of democracy.

Therefore democracy cannot be exported, neither with weapons nor with preventive wars, it has to be born and cultivated in schools with dialogue and participation.

Getting the fundamentals right and opening to the possibilities of the human spirit

Howard Gardner

Howard Gardner

Harvard School of Education, USA (video recording)

I began my involvement with the schools in Reggio about 20 years ago. I had just finished writing about the theory of multiple intelligences and was invited to come with my wife to visit Northern Italy. I had heard a bit about the schools, but was not prepared for the incredible experience of actually visiting them and getting to know the group of people associated for many years with the Reggio educational enterprise. When you are an educator as I have been, you don't have that many transforming experiences, experiences which really change your idea about what is possible.

I have always been a believer in progressive education, because that is the kind of education which I didn't have. I have always been very attracted to the idea of an education with children in which their minds and their imaginations are taken seriously, and I certainly have seen schools like that in the United States. However, the schools in Reggio were different and really expanded my notion of what is possible with young children and education. The schools on the one hand glorify things which seem to be antithetical, while on the other, they show that they are really complementary or even inseparable: the notion of being fun but also serious, of something being rooted in tradition but also being forward-looking, of something where skills are developed at the same time that imagination is cultivated. For most people, including most Americans, these values are antithetical, but not in Reggio.

Moreover, constructivism is a philosophical approach for which I have had a lot of sympathy: the notion that people must ultimately invent their own meanings, that they must construct their own minds, which did not happen for us, as we were certainly helped to construct knowledge. But I have never seen all this done with such a degree of expertise and meaningfulness as I did in these schools. Words like documentation, reflection, dialogue and the languages of children - all of these words have been given a kind of a new richness and texture by the schools. These aren't savvy words created for nothing. I could see the ideas and the work of Piaget, Montessori, Dewey, and many others. But with these authors, ideas were developed only on paper, or some were even carried out in part. Here, it went well beyond the initiative and the thoughts of an individual development. This is where I saw institutions and the community, places where the mind and the spirit of young children were taken very, very seriously. It was something that the adults cared about and were willing to invest time in, saying things like "you have talked about these things, you have argued with one another in a civil kind of way". I knew I would never be the same after visiting these schools.

The next decade, from the mid-eighties to the mid-nineties, went by very quickly. I had sporadic contacts with Reggio and attended the exhibition entitled "The hundred languages of children" when it came to the United States to New York and Boston. I participated in films about the schools, I worked with the Newsweek magazine when the schools were selected as the most outstanding in the world, and then when the National Learning Centre (part of the Washington Children's Museum) decided to build a preschool based on the Reggio ideas. I was very pleased to have worked as a catalyst in that process. I also noticed by that time that Reggio was really acquiring an international reputation which it did not have in the early eighties. The schools were already known in Sweden and in a few other places, but by the middle of the nineties, they were very well-known through much of the world.

When leaders like Carlina and Amelia came to Washington to the National Model Early Learning Centre, and when Lella came to Harvard and spoke at Project Zero, they typically began with a fairly long theoretical exposition of the way in which Reggio thought about children and education. I kept saying to myself: this is not the way we do it in America. When you are working with educators of young children, you are very practical and start up with what to do on Monday morning and so on. I was pretty sure I was right, but they paid no attention to me and in fact I think they were right because they were giving a "new" message. If you only look at the technique, or the strategy, or even the slides, you are not going to understand the deeply different way of thinking about the developing mind of a child, the community in the school, or the nature of projects. So I became convinced that it was really necessary to begin to get into the ideas very early on, and not take a cookbook approach on how to make a good school based on the Reggio school.

I was completely unprepared for Loris Malaguzzi's death ten years ago. It came as a shock to me and I gather it came as a shock to the people in Reggio Emilia as well. Since I cared about this precious experiment in childhood education, I thought that maybe it would fall apart after his death. I feared that maybe he was the glue that was holding it together, that it would be all fractionalized, and that there would be different schools or even a paralysis following the loss of such a charismatic leader. So I approached a foundation (which was anonymous at the time but not anymore) called "The Atlantic Philanthropies Business" and told them that there were these wonderful schools in Northern Italy. I said I thought that they were terrific, but that the person who led them had died suddenly, and that it would great if they could give them some help. The project officers at the Atlantic Philanthropies were sympathetic with what I said but knew nothing about the schools in Reggio Emilia. Moreover, they were not in the habit of giving money abroad, and so they said: "Well Howard, if you think these schools are a good investment and you can come up with a project and work with them, then we can give them some support". To be honest, I had not thought of this, as I do not consider myself a particularly selfless person; but in fact my objective for Reggio was quite selfless and I did not have any personal goals in mind - it just seemed an interesting opportunity. So I talked with my colleagues, Mara Krechevsky and Steve Seidel, over this business and asked them: "Would you like to do a project with these schools, would you like to get to know them better, and have them get to know us better?" Pretty soon it clicked – we got a sizeable grant for three years, which has since been renewed for us to be able to work more intimately with the schools in Reggio Emilia. This has been an incredibly important experience for me and my colleagues. We had the privilege of visiting Reggio several times over the last couple of years until the project was carried through. Two different organizations with two different histories, two different institutions - Project Zero and Reggio Schools - both about forty years of age and both having had a few changes in personnel and leadership; yet it would be misleading to say that this was an easy collaboration. Each of us had a strong view on how to do things, how we thought about things, and the right way to collaborate, to write books, to use terminology, to analyze and so on. The collaboration was rocky for the first few years, but not enough for anyone to say: "This is a mistake, let's stop it". But I think a lot of us said: "How can we get this to work better?" I think we succeeded, because as you get to know people better, you get to trust them and it is easier to have a relationship. I think we also succeeded because we discovered in some way that our expertise was more complementary than not different. For example, there is no question that when it comes to understanding and knowing how to work with children and how to help to educate them, Reggio was light years ahead of us and of what we have known in the United States. On the other hand, we were able to talk about what it was that Reggio did to make it so distinctive, in such a way that other people could understand it. We were able to translate it into stimulus that was familiar to others, whether they were preschool educators in America, administrators and policy makers in America, or educators in other parts of the world. I think that in many ways people in Reggio were too close to their own practice, so the way Project Zero has managed to put this into words and metaphors, to organize it in terms of key ideas, fits very nicely with Reggio's expertise. I now see Project Zero as part of an international network of preschool figures, of preschool doers, of individuals who have been enormously influenced by Reggio. We set up an "invisible college" in the United States where people involved were in touch with one another while the rest of the world did not know it. Thanks to Reggio Children and other initiatives in the last ten years, I think the Invisible College is now very visible and the friends of Reggio all over the world know one another and know what makes this experience possible to carry out, as well as the significance of organizing events like this.

I just want to make few comments before closing. One is that we philosophers in the United States took note of the fact that the government in Reggio Emilia and in the Emilia Romagna area has had Communists for many years. It has certainly been very socialistic in its ideas, and these are words which do not have much consonance in America. It is important to say that communist ideas about capitalism grew out of a critique of a society where everything was based upon markets and profits (and I must say I am very sympathetic to this critique). Yet this is clearly one of the reasons why Emilia Romagna is a successful part of the world, because it is where there is economic prosperity. And wherever there are resources, people can decide to use them for educational purposes. So in that sense, it is a tribute to capitalism as well as a critique of capitalism. But what strikes me much more than the economic aspects of capitalism are the issues of social capital, human capital, and psychological capital, in what is called communal capital, which anybody who visits Reggio repeatedly, as I have done over the years, gets to see. It is not just that food is good here and that the industry and technology work, but there is also a tremendous investment of time and effort in the human condition, in the moulding of children, in the helping them to grow, in the building up of a civil society of institutions that help those who are less fortunate, such as educational institutions, art institutions and cultural institutions. These are sustained not only because there

is money there, but because people really care and are willing to devote their time to it. When people talk about transporting the Reggio model, which is always the first question when you tell people about something new, anybody who knows about Reggio knows that there is no way in which you can snap your fingers and replicate it elsewhere. You cannot imitate it. At best you can reinvent it on your own soil. I personally think it is impossible to reinvent it without a lot of capital, and here I am really focusing on the psychological capital, the social capital, the human capital, the cultural capital and the communal capital, like any kind of economic capital.

I must say that the Reggio model is very attractive almost anywhere I go in the world, but there is only a minority of people who really believe that they can make it happen. They either say: "Well that's Italian, we cannot do it here", or "It takes too much time and money to do it", or "We too care about kids picking up basic skills and mastering A B C, so that they are prepared to go to a very academic kind of school. But we cannot afford have these kids playing with one another and doing silly projects about rainbows, shoes or water fountains for birds in the park." I believe that the ideas about education in Reggio are the correct ones: they are the best possible ideas I know of for young children. But I also believe that it will take decades, if not centuries, to take what is a minority view all over the world and make it more of a majority view. I remember what a famous anthropologist once said: "Never condemn a small group of people who get together to discuss something new: nothing important in the world has ever happened in any other way". Reggio is a place where forty years ago a small number of people got together to discuss something new and important. If you think about what has happened in the growth of Reggio ideas over the last forty years, it is truly astounding.

If my predictions were wrong and there were more schools like the ones in Reggio in a few years time, this would undoubtedly be a great step ahead in the quality of the life of mankind. But I am afraid to say that my caution is probably more credible, because the resistances right now in Italy against these ideas and practices never disappear, because the struggle for the right to education for children is never easy. The right to education is respect for life, for the life of the mind, for the potential in children and for human rights, including the rights for a peaceful life, a life without violent conflict. This is an important part of the Reggio view as well, but it is often ignored by people who take too much of an instrumental view and say: "Well, for what are you doing on page two, we don't have the right kind of materials for a proper atelier". The model I am talking about needs not only that kind of human capital, but also really believes in the sacredness of human life from the youngest point. So let me close with two statements: one, in Reggio Emilia you get the fundamentals right and at the same time you open to the possibilities of the human spirit; and two - I repeat once more - in Reggio Emilia you get the fundamentals right and at the same time you open to the possibilities of the human spirit.

Thank you.

An ocean of doubts and many hopes

Irene Balaguer

I would like to say a few words about Loris Malaguzzi, his work, his thought and on what his example has meant for us, as infant teachers. Our voice is the voice of the practical side, of those who, day after day, have to face up to the challenge of teaching, the challenge of schooling, the absorbing challenge of sharing the uncertainty of the future and learning.

I have divided my paper into two parts. In the first part, I will speak briefly of our relationship with Loris Malaguzzi and the influence of the pedagogy of Reggio on our situation. In the second part, I will try to share with you some of our doubts, concerns and hopes.

Malaguzzi the master and his relationship with us

We first learned about Malaguzzi at the end of the 1970s, at a decisive time for our country: democracy had only shortly been established and it was a time when everything had to be done and we thought that everything was possible. We were living in a very special climate, full of enthusiasm and optimism. It was this atmosphere, I think, that seduced Malaguzzi.

Our friend Biel Dalmau was the first of us to visit Reggio. He came back to Barcelona fascinated by Malaguzzi and the work he was doing in the nursery schools and pre-schools of that town that nobody heard of.

And so, I think that our meeting took place at a magic moment, full of enthusiasm, in a period when, in Reggio Emilia, there was the fervour of a new pedagogical experience which, through dialogue, aimed to transform society itself. This was a time when we were plunged into the popular wave that nurtured our hopes after 40 years of dictatorship. I think that I can say, in the intimacy of this Conference, that very soon we became sincerely fond of one another.

Loris Malaguzzi was a sincere man who appeared as he was: generous, curious, demanding, rigorous, creative,

Irene Balaguer
Association Rosa Sensat, Spain

imaginative, intelligent and entertaining and who was enthusiastic about many things! He loved eating in good company; he appreciated good food, he loved the Catalan cream dessert, he loved people, in particular he loved watching them and whenever he came to Barcelona, he would walk up and down the Ramblas, that part of the city which is always alive, where different people and customs come together.

In those years, Malaguzzi was concentrated on his eyes: he was obsessed by eyes, eyes as an element of provocation, as transgression, eyes as a challenge, eyes to learn something new, eyes to make visible the counterpoint to the verbalism of traditional schools which dominated the educational panorama, to go against convention and above all, as routine practice, eyes to make us wake up. It was at this time that he was preparing the first exhibition "If the eye jumps over the wall" together with the pedagogical work of the schools in Reggio, with the idea of the laboratory as an element generating the new way of understanding education concerning early infancy. He brought out the skill of the child, through the provocation of making us think of this child, whose limits we know so little about.

In his eyes and his view of reality there is something that has always made me think of Picasso. At times, there are those who think they can recognise in Picasso certain elements characteristic of Cézanne, Lautrec, Goya or Gris, but it is always Picasso. And in Malaguzzi too, there are those who can recognise Pestalozzi, Vigotski or Freinet, but it is always Malaguzzi.
Geniuses like Picasso and Malaguzzi have been inspired by the works of others to do their own work, but recreating and creating a continual process, always staying themselves.

Both of them, Malaguzzi and Picasso, have shown us reality from a new point of view that we had never imagined before. They way they had of looking at everyday life allowed us to see the visible and the invisible of every situation and every individual.

The exhibition "If the eye jumps over the wall" highlights Malaguzzi's view, the new pedagogy that came into being in the nursery schools and pre-schools of Reggio. The Exhibition was shown in Barcelona in 1984, in 1987 in Madrid and in Palma de Mallorca. It had a clear impact on all these cities, both for the level of attendance and for the effect of dynamism which it had on the world of education and politics, becoming a reference in meetings between teachers and in the major debates on education which were being held in the country on the Law on Education which was being outlined.

The participation of Malaguzzi, Mariano Dolci and Carla Rinaldi in the Rosa Sensat Summer Schools was a possibility of following the evolution of his thought year by year, his hopes and disillusions on school, politics and politicians, on Reggio and Barcelona and, lastly, on the world. There are increasing numbers of universities and other teacher training institutions that want to know and teach your thought.

All these initiatives are accompanied by cultural visits to Reggio Emilia, with the aim of directly getting to know the schools and activities performed there, through periods of study with you and amongst you to be able to gradually follow the process of pedagogical creation and thought. There are hundreds or perhaps thousands of teachers in my country who have paid and continue to pay attention to your process of pedagogical construction. With the passing of the years, perhaps we will be able to say that a network of political and pedagogical friendships and partnerships has been woven around you.

Despite this long-standing relationship, the presence of your pedagogy in the Spanish and Catalonian situations is veiled and difficult to identify on first sight. In the first place and, without any doubt at all, this is due to the enormous pedagogical-conceptual, historic, political distances and differences in resources separating our countries. The compromise with infancy and education is very weak or weakened by the lack of people such as those you have here and in many other towns and regions of Italy capable of creating and fighting to transform reality.
In the second place, the influence does not meet the canons of reproduction, transposition or imitation: therefore it is difficult to identify this presence.

Undoubtedly, the situation in Spain, which can be more clearly identified with the pedagogy of Reggio, is represented by the nursery schools of the Municipal Area of Pamplona, where the cooperation of individuals and institutions has united political and pedagogical action. Their work takes all its inspiration from the thought and work of Malaguzzi.

Alfredo Hoyuelos was didactic director of the laboratories of the town's schools for over twenty years and made a decisive contribution to generating the dynamic pedagogy of Reggi that he knows very well and highly appreciates. It is to him that we owe the full compilation of the thought of Malaguzzi, thanks to his faithful, rigorous and colossal work, in an exceptional thesis for a Ph.D, which will spread knowledge about the person and work of the educationalist of the 21st century, Malaguzzi.

All the other influences are more veiled, but they are nevertheless present in the thoughts and actions of hundred, or perhaps thousands of teachers who have understood the dimension and the compromise with infancy and society that your pedagogy demands. And I am certain in saying this, because I know our situation through visiting schools, summer schools, continuous education of discussion groups, through difficult strikes than many teachers in Spain have put up with and will still have to put up with to defend the dignity of school for the youngest members of society. Because, as if on principle, they are capable of not being attracted by better salaries, with the objective of keeping a model of a school that respects children and is in constant dialogue with families.

In 1990, Malaguzzi wrote a letter to Marta Mata and myself. Marta Mata is the main referent in Spain for Pedagogical renewal and the defence of state schooling. The letter was due to two major events for the education of small children.

The first event concerned the approval of the Law on education in which education from 0 to 6 years was acknowledged as the first level of the new Educational System of the country. Malaguzzi knew that laws do not change reality, but he also knew that they are essential to transform it. He envied us from this point of view. it was as if with it a collective dream was coming true, in that the right of children to education was acknowledged and the parameters of the quality of schooling were being marked out.

The other subject in his letter was the creation of the magazine "Infancia" in Spanish, a language that gave us the possibility to dialogue with a very important part of the world, with the whole of Latin America, an area that he thought highly of. He was perhaps even more enthusiastic about this subject and he set us new challenges.

Both pieces of news filled us with hope, both went beyond the limits.

Apart from all these past and present stories of the influence that he has had and that the political and pedagogical reality of Reggio has in the world and in the worlds each of us comes from, there is a clear invitation to think, from the perspective of the future, on the multiple situations of infancy, education and school.

An ocean of doubts and many hopes

All of us now know that the hopes of the last decades of the twentieth century have undergone great and rapid transformation.

Today, we live immersed in a multitude of transformations regarding values, economy, science, social life, politics, speed and quantity of information, technology, local and global dimension, the temporal dimension...

Our world today suffocates us, its immensity can influence our capacity of interpreting and response, at least mine.
Our global and local world, of majorities and minorities, immobilises us, because we all know that in the world of majorities:

One and a half thousand million children live on less than one Euro a day. Fifteen million children under five die every year because they do not get medical treatment.
More than one hundred million live in the streets.
Four hundred million are exploited in terrible working conditions.

And we also know that in the world of minorities:

The commercialisation of childhood is on the increase, with childhood being shamefully exploited through the publicity by the various sects where sexual abuse of minors is a right of adults.

This is some data on our world which at times we cannot understand. It is a world where it would seem that we have all become deaf, blind and dumb.

About a year ago, a young friend who is not a teacher and has no link at all with the world of education, visited Mali. When he came back, he told us, astonished and curious at the same time: "I visited people who live in one of the poorest regions in the world and I met generous people and a people where children are happy".

Last week a teacher friend sent us this postcard from her journey in Guatemala and Chiapas, where there are also some of the poorest people in Latin America. On the postcard she writes: "There are children here everywhere: they skip, jump...and look happy". Why do situations in these worlds surprise us so much? What should happen in our world which is apparently so rich, where everything is so plentiful but that is unable to give an answer or that asks questions on the most essential things in life? What will "rich" mean?

A world where, whilst international organisations like UNICEF, in its 2001 Report on the situation of children in the world, draws attention to responsibility saying: "Early childhood should receive priority attention from governments, expressed in laws, policies and resources. In spite of this, these are the years when children receive least attention and this fact is a tragedy both for the children and for the countries involved".

In some countries such as Spain, the laws conceived by the government are a further example of the barbarity surrounding us. The Spanish law on education which Malaguzzi was so enthusiastic about in 1990 has been repealed. New Spanish law on education abandons schools to the market, making private management the apotheosis and the model to be followed, thus exalting competitivity. In this way, schools are seen as a business, not as a service to society and it is the negation of the competence and social right of all children to education.

This is a very serious fact and an attack that we all understand in its enormity, but more than anything, this law confuses inculcating, transmitting and imposing with what education really is. Education knows that only a free person, a free child can decide to learn and to grow. Perhaps what is at stake today is the existence of the condition of children.

But we know, because we have been with them and we have talked to them, what they ignore: that children cannot be reduced to our desires on them. We know that children put up resistance to our constrictions as powerful adults. This is what the current law proposes with its narrow and reductive vision of school and education.

And so, stating today that childhood really exists is not something to be taken for granted but the means to resist the temptation of fabricating a child rather than educating him/her. This is a permanent temptation that runs through the entire history of humanity.

And it is at exactly this point that your work and our role alongside you takes its strength. Precisely because we offer an education where children are the actors, individual people, who commit themselves without having to be dominated or trained.

The educational habit we share assumes accepting education as a meeting point, accepting the child as resistance, because we are aware that if a child exists, he/she resists. We cannot know what goes on inside a child, inside his/her mind: he/she escapes the power of adult imposition.

If this resistance actually exists, as teachers, we have to learn to do things together and doing things together with children means entering into the pedagogical moment when we, as teachers, will have stopped making the child an object for our satisfaction, we will have stopped being invasive with the child and we will learn with them in the precise way as defined by Janusz Korczak.

This approach of education as dialogue, as dialogues, means accepting that the child and children have a present and that they are people with full rights to live in their present.
These laws negate this present. These laws do not accept that the child, however small, is a person with full rights, an unfinished person if we like, like any other living person. Not even adults can consider themselves totally complete. Because a complete man is not a man: it is an image, someone without any concerns or doubts: it is a dead person.

But real people, children and adults, are complex and incomplete people at the same time and as is our understanding, they are always in a continuous process of change and knowledge.

From this point of view, the orientation of the new laws on education, at least the one concerning us, violates the right to education to the extent that children's right to education is first of all the right to live at their own pace, to live in a context free of the threats that hover over any pupil. At this point, the positive value that is given in your pedagogy and in your schools to learning through mistakes is of fundamental importance, similar to the value taken on by error in the process of scientific knowledge.

A position and a way of acting that is far from those who talk about closed curricula, final objectives and coercive evaluations, who see mistakes as something which is not profitable and only a waste of time. It is the threat of those who prefer to see them immobile and anchored to their ignorance.

We all know that exercising the right to education requires the presence of a capable adult, an adult with whom dialogue can be started, with whom knowledge can be built up. An adult who has to be evaluated and this point is also negated by the law.

I am aware of all the limitations that I have tried to consider, present in the scenario that concerns me.

It is precisely in these situations that I always wonder what Malaguzzi would have thought, what he would have said... he who always pushed himself further in questions and knew how to guide us to finding answers.

But, although we feel orphans, we have to try, we have to look ahead and to do what we have learned from him. Let's talk about it, discuss things together and perhaps we will find the way to ask questions and begin to draw up answers.

He showed us, with his way of behaving as a teacher, that you have to be rebellious, insubordinate and revolutionary. He showed us that it is impossible to teach without having trust, without hoping and without becoming indignant over the condition today of the most precious asset of humanity: its children who are condemned to suffer aggressions of all kinds. Malaguzzi was a rebel, a man who could not tolerate violence on children. He could not bear physical and psychological violence but nor could he bear the violence of the institutions.

Josep Palau i Fabre, a well known scholar of Picasso, who from my point of view has many things in common with Malaguzzi and his work, says that, just as fishermen with their nets, so Ariadne spread her golden net from one end of the Labyrinth to the author.

He asks: what does a finished work mean? When we say that someone is finished, we mean that he is dead. In his works, he always leaves a window open that lets us breathe and continue to live... In his works he has always taken into account this important lesson on creation. All of us have to be able to continue stretching the golden net from one end of the Labyrinth to the other.

We have to learn to weave a vast and close-knit network and we have to learn to rebel.

The child is the "first citizen"

Carla Rinaldi

"Man is meeting"
"a part"
"a question on a science which never ceases to hope
in us".

I thought this sentence by Gregory Bateson was a lovely metaphor, capable of synthesising and expressing the life and philosophy of Loris Malaguzzi.

There are in fact several ways of narrating the work of a scholar, of a philosopher, of a researcher; of a man like Loris Malaguzzi.
Although perhaps (as S. Manghi says) there are really only two: one is to think of the man and his work as if they were here in front of us, objectified and complete; the other is to think of the work in relation to ourselves, part of us, work which also speaks of us, continue and evolve with us and in us, and from which we take on meaning and responsibility.

In this phase of history, where the news too often describes and exalts the success of the individual over the group, the victory of the solitary leader saved by a miracle, people's uniqueness as an element of separation and isolation rather than a strength and resource for dialogue, the truest, most sincere and relevant way I can think of paying homage to Malaguzzi is to speak of his extraordinary ability for promoting that sense of belonging, the educational project, that "we" which has been capable of crossing boundaries, embracing dreams and building hope through encounter, through close exchange, through the angers and joys of transforming dialogue.
Crossing boundaries: Malaguzzi loved to cross boundaries, he loved to inhabit the border areas.
Not boundaries which have been established once and for all, or defined a priori; but boundaries perceived as places for meeting and exchange, where knowledge and action pursue and feed each other in succession.

Together with him we shared many journeys and crossed many boundaries. We learned the "art" of CREATIVE TRANSCRIPTION as Malaguzzi loved to

Carla Rinaldi
University of Modena e Reggio Emilia

define it. This helped us not to accept the boundary of his death as a limit or the dramatic interruption of processes and pathways constructed together.

I still remember the pain, the struggle ten years ago in imagining us existing without his presence or continuing to seek the path without his guidance. I still remember my sadness and difficulty and that of colleagues in infant-toddler centres and schools, but mostly I remember the determination in our wish to carry on feeling and being "WE".

We have tried to keep some values constant even with rapid variations in strategies and objectives. We have tried to elaborate an educational project which is also made of slower rhythms when most of contemporary society seems oriented towards brevity and a constantly fluctuating instability.

We committed ourselves to building a present which is aware of the past and responsible towards the future, and we especially tried to consolidate our awareness that we were the protagonists of a project which was not only about early childhood education, but about people, about mankind, and this awareness helped us to understand that it was and still is necessary to make choices in pedagogy but in ethics and values too.

Pedagogy like school is not neutral, it takes sides, it participates in deep and vital ways in the definition of this project whose central theme is not mankind, but his relations with the world, his being the world, his feeling of INTERDEPENDENCE with what is other than himself.

So pedagogy implies choices, and choosing does not mean deciding what is right compared to what is wrong. Choosing means having the courage of our doubts, of our uncertainties, it means participating in something we take responsibility for.

We made these choices thanks to exchange and debate with colleagues and friends here in Reggio Emilia, in Italy and throughout the world. I would like to express my and our gratitude for this to all those who have supported, shared and also criticised our choices.

With their help we have constructed our identity, an identity which is open to change. We have constructed the differences that we feel now more than ever, to be the value we can offer, aware and responsible for the fact that this way we are constructing a true concept of belonging.
In fact we are all connected, wherever we work, even in such geographically and culturally distant and dif-

ferent contexts, to the same community of destiny, to a new and complex planetary anthropology.

What choices can I offer you for attention to try and give you the wider meaning that derives from them?
Surely the first is that concerning the image of the child and the theory of learning that we have referred to for guiding our experience, our journey.
It is widely known that our choice or better, one of the focal points of our philosophy, is the image of a COMPETENT CHILD.
"What competencies is the child is in possession of?" we asked ourselves, and to understand this we tried to meet the child, see him, to understand him, to enter into a dialogue with him.
A child is competent in forming relations, in communicating – I would dare to say in living.
Each child born is a "could be" of humanity, he is a possibility, the beginning of a hope, and is deeply influenced by the levels of awareness, the will, the courage and the politics of the country receiving him.

Children are not only our future, which we invest in by oppressing their dreams and freedom to be something other than we would wish them to be; they are our present.
The child is not a citizen of the future, he is the "first citizen", a statement which for me is completely without rhetoric.
The child is a bearer, here and now, of rights, of values, of culture: the culture of childhood.
He is not only our knowledge about childhood, but childhood's knowledge of how to be and how to live.
It is our historical responsibility not only to affirm this but to CREATE CULTURAL, SOCIAL, POLITICAL AND EDUCATIONAL CONTEXTS, which are able to receive children and dialogue with their potential for constructing HUMAN RIGHTS.
These are physical contexts but also mental contexts which require; the deconstruction and overcoming of our preconceptions about childhood, the social reconstruction of a new culture of childhood, the construction of a new culture of mankind and a new identity for ourselves (educators, parents and adults).
Children's ways of interpreting and experiencing give us paradigms for thought, that is to say, different ways of feeling emotions and thinking which are disruptive and inconvenient because they are de-structured in comparison to familiar ways.

And in an era of globalisation where we are coming to redefine the very concept of mankind, starting/restarting from children, from their generous humanity, from trying to give new answers to their requests for sense, might make it possible for us now more than in the past, to have the courage to rewrite a new complex anthropology.

I am not proposing a romantic approach, or an image of childhood which comes close to the creation of a cathartic world, but I would like to emphasise this strong feeling of a change in model, that western thinking must adjust so that we can find, as never in the past, vital energy from the relationship and dialogue with children and childhood.

Built around the interpretation of this concept of "competent child" was the sharing of the value of interaction and dialogue as essential qualities defining our relations with children and adults, with the city itself and with others in general and which had structured implications for our choices.

The greatest effort Malaguzzi led us to make was in finding forms of organisation which were not only consistent with the theoretical declarations we had assumed, but able to guarantee the vitality, the bringing to crisis point of that same organisation and its self-renewal.
Organisation which would guarantee us change, and sustain a logic not of production but of reproduction, that is to say – generative creativity.
Organisation capable of listening and sustaining creativity up to the point where it takes on the value of risk and of adventure.
There were trade unionist friends, politicians, people of good sense who understood that for an organisation or an educational system to be such, it cannot take on the logic of production and standardisation but must be capable of embracing the surprises and disruptions of organisation built up on a daily basis.
The "pedagogy of relations", as Malaguzzi loved to define the pedagogy enacted in our schools, found that exchange was easy and immediate with that area of architecture defined as relational. This dialogue and exchange has been particularly fruitful and has never been exhausted exactly because today – more than a dialogue – it has become a common research project, not only around school architecture but around children and adults and their ways of inhabiting the world.
In the same way we chose to dialogue with all those people in various areas of discipline (psychology, human sciences, biology, neurology, art and design) who agreed to carry out research with us, constructing questions together, experiencing journeys of research together which were respectful of each person's role, without preconceived hierarchies between academic knowledge and the knowledge of operators.
A journey which was also playful and entertaining, surprising and doubtful, because when researching into the things of children, it is really the children who must be the main protagonists of that research.
A researching school: a theme close to Malaguzzi's heart and ours – and to the hearts of others.

I need to cite this point in order to introduce a theme which represents a characteristic feature, and one of the most criticised, of our experience: *the construction of vocabulary* often used as an alternative to more usual vocabulary.
We can understand this but it was a fundamental element in the construction of our identity, above all because it was a way of constructing common values and meanings, of constructing choices, in order to be "we" and be able to offer this "open identity".
Supporting this there has always been humour, when there is a strong risk of being too dogmatic.
It is humour which often guides our criticism and self-criticism, and this too has been learned from children who as we know, are capable of being extremely humorous.
We have tried to cross boundaries but also to inhabit them.
In the face of historic antonyms such as work-play, reality-imagination we propose emotion and knowledge, creativity and rationality, syllabus-progettazione, teaching-research, individual-group, rigid science-plastic science.
We have tried to observe children and to observe ourselves with children.
We became aware and wanted to make visible that this dualistic way of thinking does not belong to children or to adults but to those who believe that "scientific" means without emotion, without passion, without heart; those who believe that it is truer and more objective.
We have been able to see instead how reason and emotion, learning and pleasure, fatigue and joy, oneself and others, are not only capable of cohabiting together, but of reciprocally generating each other, supported by the strong force which comes from creative – and thus knowing – freedom.
The freedom of the unknown, of doubt, of the unfamiliar; a freedom children have if it is not restricted.

With these premises our choices become obvious around a problematic nucleus which has always been the subject of debate: the teaching-learning relationship.
This is what Malaguzzi wrote on the subject: "The aim of teaching is not to produce learning but to produce the conditions for learning, this is the focal point, the quality of the learning".
The key tool and structure we had for consolidating this statement was documentation. Documentation, cited in

many international texts on pedagogy as a tool for archiving and/or for the subsequent reconstruction of journeys already completed, is given an original interpretation in our work which places it within the process of teaching and therefore of learning.

Documentation "in process", enacted and interpreted during research and not simply at the end, can guide the direction of the journey itself and encourage relations between children's structures for knowledge and for subjects (the concept of progettazione/syllabus).

Documentation then is seen as a tool for teaching but also as a structure for epistemology, in that by favouring memory and reflection it can modify teaching and knowledge processes in children and in the group of children and teachers.

So then, reciprocal teaching and learning.

If the teacher, besides her role of support and cultural mediation knows how to observe, make documentation and interpret, she will achieve her highest potential for learning and teaching.

Recent reflections, shared with colleagues working in the Reggio experience and others make it possible to bring your attention to some further areas of research we are exploring more deeply:

– documentation processes, in the way we have described them, are by their nature also processes of evaluation (they give value, to elements considered significant by making them visible)

– the documents produced are tools for evaluation and self-evaluation. They are an opportunity for reflection, interpretation, dialogue, negotiation and connection of theory to practice. A strategy for evaluation understood as THE CONSTRUCTION OF SHARED MEANING.

Certainly for us documentation, or better, the concept of visibility and sharing was also an important cultural and political opportunity which gave us the strength to cross other boundaries and start up new exchanges.

Documentation also revealed itself to be an effective form for constructing group identity, history and memories for starting up participated journeys.

All this required – requires – time.

We chose, we sought to give time to the children and to ourselves.

We were speaking of the concept of participation.

The schools of Reggio Emilia which were born of a true process of popular participation, together with other Italian experiences, are a declaration of participation by families, who constitute part of their identity.

Over the years it would be revealed that participation is at the essence of processes of learning and identity in children and adults; it is a way of being a child, an educator, a parent. Participation then, is a common journey which makes it possible to construct the sense of belonging to a community.

This is a time of great discussion about reasons for the failure of participatory democracy in schools and elsewhere. We feel the obligation to share difficult aspects with others, but also to declare with force the irrevocability of participation as an identifying feature of the very concept of school, education and democracy.

Each individual, in fact, expresses a unique cultural potential which schools and educational institutions must not only recognise and protect, they must also understand that they can only do this by building a context of interaction and exchange between these different uniquenesses.

Uniqueness too manifests itself, is nourished, only through exchange.

In this way we realise that schools assume the character of an agorà [meeting place], where a plurality of opinions and points of view guarantees secularity and where "being educational" means they can be places for elaborating culture.

Cultural elaboration not only of a culture of childhood but above all of culture produced by childhood.

Participation in the debate around themes such as " the relationship between language and thought", "the relationship between areas of knowledge", "interdisciplinarity" and "the community" was probably the starting point for one of Malaguzzi's most important works: *the theory of the hundred languages and the atelier*.

Much has been written and much declared through our exhibition, videos and other material, but I feel it is necessary to specify that the hundred languages of children is not only a metaphor for crediting children and adults with a hundred, a thousand creative and communicative potentials.

In our opinion the hundred languages represents a strategy for construction of concepts and consolidation of understanding, but above all it is a declaration concerning the equal dignity and importance of all languages, which has become more and more obviously necessary for the construction of knowledge.

There is also the conviction, born of several years of experience, reflection and exchange, that creativity and poetics exist in every language, including those we define as scientific, as well as a strong aesthetic element (beauty) which acts as a connecting element in and between concepts.

Beauty orients and attracts.

It is the task of teaching (assisted by documentation) to sustain the meeting of languages which are enriched by exchange with other languages and discover their own limits, their own silences and their own omissions.

It is beauty, "the attraction of "being a part"", it is the aesthetic of knowledge, Bateson would say.

It is an ECOLOGY OF LANGUAGES

An ecology where technological language can be of fundamental support if we let the computer and other forms of technology become tools, media capable not simply of adding but of multiplying, able that is, to create something new and unpredictable. It is our hope that they will be able to act as a support to creativity.

The atelier is a metaphorical space in schools which taken as a whole aim to support the development of communication and of the hundred languages.

I believe there is distinction to be made: the difference that I sense exists between atelier and studio workshops. It is not a "lack of distinction in language" it is a difference in concept and pedagogy.

Workshops both outside and inside schools are much talked of today: and the debate is open.

It is my suspicion that for many people workshops are something which go beyond school and beyond academic knowing in the same way that creative languages go beyond knowledge.

In Reggio Emilia the atelier has come to be developed more and more as a metaphor – not for creative languages – but for a strategy of knowing, a way of structuring knowledge and organising learning.

We do not have schools and the atelier with the hundred languages like a kind of "removable appendage". We have "schools of research" in which the atelier is an essential component in the sense that it is the essence of school as research.

We have been discussing children together, but we have always put children, boys, girls, adolescents, men and women together.

These are thoughts which childhood has inspired, but childhood is not a separate phase of life or of human identity.

Childhood is the loveliest metaphor for describing the possibilities of mankind, on the understanding that we let it exist, that we recognise it and that we cease all these processes of acceleration and cultural aping, which in denying childhood destroy not childhood but man.

I am drawing to the close.

I apologise for the limits and partial nature of these reflections.

I have made choices of content and tried to use language which might be understood by the hundreds of people here present from many different cultures and pedagogies.

I trust the visits in infant-toddler centres and preschools today and the sessions tomorrow with the task of exploring more deeply the themes I have discussed.

In each school you will find traces which are common to all the others; a fragment of the whole in each one.

That is Reggio Emilia: a kaleidoscope which mirrors and in which we can be mirrored (Batesonian self reflection).

One thing that I hope I have been able to communicate is the intellectual honesty and passion of this experience and its protagonists near and far.

Malaguzzi never concealed his great aspirations, hopes and expectations of teachers.

Those who knew him well will also remember how exacting, severe and rigorous he was (first and foremost with himself) but they also know that this was the outward sign of his deep respect and gratitude towards teachers.

A respect which Malaguzzi always transformed into tangible gestures – battles shared, sweeping passions, generous public demonstrations remember him well, and into small but essential details of everyday life (trusting in children meant and means trusting in teachers).

So respect for their intelligence, ability and possibilities; a firm invitation to be the protagonists together with children in educational, cultural and political choices.

Like the great respect he had for the intelligence of families who he looked to full of hope and optimism.

I hope that together we too have been capable of offering this respect and trust and will continue to be capable of offering it, though we face a more difficult and contradictory future.

That is why dedicating a day to Loris Malaguzzi means also dedicating it to the teachers and schools of Reggio Emilia.

Schools as spaces for political and ethical practice

Peter Moss

I first visited Reggio more than a decade ago. But it is only during the last 6 years or so, after the death of Loris Malaguzzi, that I have begun to gain some understanding of his work and the importance of the experience of Reggio Emilia and its schools. This relatively short collaboration has been invaluable. For the creative thinking and innovative practice that are the hallmark of Malaguzzi and Reggio have helped me to find a way out of problems that were proving perplexing.

Throughout the 1990s, for example, the concept of quality and its measurement troubled me: how could quality accommodate subjectivity and values, context and multiple perspectives? The answer turned out to be that it could not. Subjectivity, values, context and multiple perspectives required another concept of evaluation, which might be termed meaning making; and a different sort of tool, pedagogical documentation. And where do you find meaning making and pedagogical documentation not just talked about but practiced? In the life of Loris Malaguzzi and the work of Reggio's municipal schools.

So Malaguzzi and Reggio helped me get beyond quality. And now they provide inspiration again. Gunilla Dahlberg and I have been working on a book which starts with a question. What would it mean were schools to be understood, first and foremost, as spaces or sites for political and ethical practice? The need to ask the question arises because schools today are so often conceptualised as, first and foremost, places of technical practice for promoting linear development and transmitting a defined body of knowledge: what Malaguzzi dismissed as a 'small pedagogy'.

We live at a time when, globally, unprecedented attention is paid to early childhood and to the development of services for young children and their families. This is welcome: but it also puts me in mind of Foucault's

Peter Moss

University of London, United Kingdom

Thomas Coram Research Unit, Institute of Education University of London warning that while everything is not bad, everything is dangerous. This growing international interest in the young child brings opportunities, but it is also dangerous: it may lead to the child being more governed than ever before. For it seems to me that so much of today's discussion about early childhood, and indeed discussion about schools and other services for older children, is strongly influenced by a very particular way of thinking: that the application of the right technology to children from an early age will produce subjects who will meet the needs of neoliberal economies and advanced liberal societies, subjects who will be flexible workers, autonomous citizens and calculating consumers. A dominating discourse, inscribed with the disciplinary perspective of developmental psychology, tells us what the child should be; and an array of concepts and practices – quality, excellence, outcomes, developmentally appropriate practice to mention but a few – create a dense network of norms and the means to ensure conformity to these norms. In this way, schools become, first and foremost, places of technical practice and normalisation.

It is in this context that the thought and practice of Malaguzzi and the municipal schools of Reggio Emilia become so important. This thought and practice do not dismiss technical practices, they do not ignore matters of organisation and structure: but this thought and practice puts them in their place. Malaguzzi and Reggio insist that early childhood is first and foremost a matter of political and ethical practice: "we don't forget (says Carlina Rinaldi) that behind every solution and every organization, this means behind every school, there is a choice of values and ethics".

So for my contribution today I want to recognise and celebrate Loris Malaguzzi's contribution to this all-important, but too often neglected, political and ethical dimension. What can be more political than his question: what is your image of the child? Or Carlina Rinaldi when she says that "childhood does not exist, we create it as a society, as a public subject. It is a social, political and historical construction".

Malaguzzi was quite clear about Reggio's answer to his political question:

> One of our strengths has been to start out from a very clear, very open declaration of our ideas about the young child. It is a highly optimistic vision of the child: a child who possesses many resources at birth, and with an extraordinary potential which has never ceased to amaze us; a child with the independent means to build up its own thought processes, ideas, questions and

attempts at answers; with a high level of ability in conversing with adults, the ability to observe things and to reconstruct them in their entirety. This is a gifted child, for whom we need a gifted teacher.

And as this quotation suggests, the politics of childhood includes other political questions. Who do we think the teacher is? And how do we understand institutions of childhood, such as the school? There is, again, no single right answer to such questions. They are highly contestable, they are the stuff of politics – and Reggio has made its political choices. The teacher, in Reggio, is not a technician, certainly not a substitute mother – both still powerful images elsewhere. She is a co-constructor of knowledge and values together with children; she is a cultured and curious person, which means an inveterate border crosser; and she is a researcher, with an enquiring and critical mind – and Malaguzzi bequeathed to Reggio a belief in the importance of research, not as a separate academic activity but as an integral part of everyday life.

The way we understand the school and other institutions for children is equally important. An understanding that is very strong today is the school as an enclosure where technologies can be applied to children to produce predetermined outcomes; the metaphor is the factory, predictability and conformity the main values. Another understanding, especially strong in the English language world, is the school as a business, competing in a market to sell commodities such as care and education to individual consumers.

Reggio offers a very different understanding. The school as a public space, a place of encounter, interaction and connection between citizens young and old, and which has many possibilities – some predetermined and predictable, but many others that are not, but which instead will surprise and amaze. Reggio, too, understands its schools as public institutions, not private commodities, in a close and open relationship with their local communities, foregrounding values of democracy, solidarity and hospitality.

Malaguzzi and Reggio have also provided us with a powerful tool for making schools spaces for the practice of democratic political practice: pedagogical documentation. This method for making pedagogical work visible and therefore subject to interpretation and critique welcomes difference and confrontation, multiple perspectives and divergent interpretations. Pedagogical documentation serves several purposes: evaluation, where evaluation is understood as a democratic process of meaning making rather than the managerial assessment of quality; learning about learning, through adopting a researching approach; and making the work of the school the subject of what Nikolas Rose calls 'minor politics', a politics "concerned with the here and now, not with some fantasized future". Alfredo Hoyuelos, Malaguzzi's biographer, captures the political and ethical purpose of pedagogical documentation when he writes

> Documenting is one of the keys to Malaguzzi's philosophy. Behind the practice I believe is the ethical concept of a transparent school and transparent education…A political idea also emerges, which is what schools do must have public visibility: thus 'giving back' to the city what the city has invested in them.

I cannot leave the theme of political practice without mentioning one other way in which Malaguzzi opens up for politics. For it seems to me that he engages in what has been termed a *politics of epistemology*. He contests modernity's idea of knowledge as the objective representation of a real world, in favour of knowledge as socially constructed by each one of us in relation with others. Again I quote from Alfredo Hoyuelos:

> Malaguzzi's pedagogy is complex: 'it allows itself' subjective, divergent and independent interpretations of the world in contrast with linear and accumulative progress. It takes a sceptical position on past, present and future certainties…Its credo is that the subject constructs – with others and in democracy – her or his own epistemology, her or his own way of seeing the world: in the conviction that this represents only a partial vision with an expectation of other possible ways of seeing.

The spread of technical practice smothers the politics of epistemology. Malaguzzi and Reggio provide an oxygen supply, by insisting that the meaning of knowledge is contestable. And in *their* understanding of knowledge – as constructed, perspectival, provisional, rhizomatic – they also make into contestable and political issues concepts and tools that are today widely taken for granted as neutral and self-evident: curriculum, quality, outcomes, development.

If a school might be, first and foremost, a space for political and ethical practice, where do the ethics come in? And what ethics? In trying to understand what it might mean to conceptualise ethics as first practice in schools, Gunilla and I have had two sources of inspiration. First, the work of the Canadian Bill Readings. In his final book, the *University in Ruins*, Readings offers his vision of universities and other institutions for education and learning,

> as sites of *obligation*, as loci of *ethical practices*, rather than as sites for the transmission of scientific knowledge…. The condition of pedagogical practice is 'an infinite attention to the other'. …(and) education is this drawing out of the otherness of thought….[It is] *Listening to Thought*... Doing justice to Thought, listening to our interlocutors, means trying to hear that which cannot be said but that which tries to make itself heard".

There are two important concepts in what Readings says: the idea of schools as 'loci of ethical practices' and the idea of learning as 'listening to thought'. And both connect, I think, to Malaguzzi and Reggio. For Readings' idea of listening to thought has much in common with Reggio's concept of a 'pedagogy of listening'. And both, Gunilla and I would argue, are inscribed with a particular ethical approach: Emmanual Levinas's concept of the ethics of an encounter.

Levinas argues that there is a strong Western philosophical tradition that gives primacy to knowing. Through this will to know, we grasp the other and make the other into the same. An example is the concepts and classifications of developmental psychology, which give us as teachers or researchers possibilities to possess and 'comprehend' the child. Alterity disappears and singularity and novelty are excluded, to be replaced by 'the totalitarianism of the same'.

Working with the ethics of an encounter requires the teacher (or indeed the researcher or policy maker), in Gunilal Dahlberg's words, "to think an other whom I cannot grasp [which] is an important shift and it challenges the whole scene of pedagogy". And Reggio's 'pedagogy of listening' provides one way in which this important shift can be made. For a pedagogy of listening means listening to thought – the ideas and theories, questions and answers of children – treating thought seriously and with respect, struggling to make meaning from what is said, without preconceived ideas of what is correct or appropriate. 'A pedagogy of listening' involves an ethical relationship of openness to the Other, trying to listen to the Other from his or her own position and experience and not treating the other as the same. A 'pedagogy of listening' treats knowledge as constructed, perspectival and provisional, not the transmission of a body of knowledge which makes the Other into the same.

In writing our new book, Gunilla and I have found,

once again, that Reggio was there first: through a politics of childhood and a pedagogy of listening, they have shown what it means to make schools, first and foremost, sites for political and ethical practice. And so much of this flows from Malaguzzi's thinking: the importance he attached to democratic relationships; his readiness to embrace different perspectives and uncertainty; his appreciation of the socially constructed, provisional and complex nature of knowledge, captured in his metaphor for knowledge as a 'tangle of spaghetti'; his joy in making connections and border crossing; his openness to the unexpected and his relish for experimentation – all of which open up to a relationship of respect for the other and a desire to listen rather than grasp.

After six years of collaboration, what is my image of Reggio Emilia? Or rather images, as three come readily to mind. First, Reggio as a complex of workshops or laboratories, where children and adults are constantly experimenting, inventing and welcoming the new and unknown. Second, Reggio as an island of dissensus, a challenge to normalising tendencies in early childhood, a place that makes the familiar strange and forces us to question the taken-for-granted assumptions of dominant discourses. But not an isolated island, an island in the middle of the ocean; but part of an archipelago of islands sharing values and with frequent connections. Lastly, Reggio as an example of utopian thought and action, at a time when we increasingly find it difficult to imagine really different ways of thinking and doing.

The Portuguese social scientist, Boaventura de Sousa Santos speaks of the widespread disillusion and disenchantment in our world today, and a loss of hope in the future. We must, he argues, reinvent the future by opening up a new horizon of possibilities:

> Merely to criticize the dominant paradigm, though crucial, is not enough. We must also define the emergent paradigm, this being the really important and difficult task…The only route, it seems to me, is utopia. By utopia I mean the exploration by imagination of new modes of human possibility…and the confrontation by imagination of the necessity of whatever exists – just because it exists.

I can think of new better definition of utopia, nor of the 40 years of work in Reggio that we are celebrating at this conference. And when I think of Malaguzzi in this context, I see him as an inventor, a dissenter and an explorer, but above all as a utopian thinker and actor who could imagine new modes of human possibility and had an unquenchable hope for the future.

An experience of a community

Susanna Mantovani

I met Loris Malaguzzi for the first time in 1971 at the Conference on the social management of nursery schools. I was about to graduate in philosophy and at my faculty in Milan I had lived through the years when there had been an explosion, at times violent and always with great vitality, in young people of interest in and commitment, although not always constructive, to everything that could be considered social.

What was significant for me was going from interests of a theoretical and philosophical type to looking for the articulation of knowledge and theories in real life and above all in human development, in childhood and in schools.

It was the first time I had encountered educational experiences rooted in the community, which were intrinsically pedagogical and at the same time political, the discovery of the community and popular origins of schools as contexts where educational responsibility was exercised not only individually as parents or teachers, but also as citizens and the discovery of council-run nursery schools as *public squares* or as *agorà* of pedagogical creativity and democratic practice. It was the school of the school-city committees, of the "social management" as it was then translated at national level in the decrees of execution of 1974 and partly bureaucratised, whilst in Reggio and in some other municipal experiences it continued to evolve profoundly and led to the practice and reflection on **participation** as a foundation for educational practices and for the shared definition of educational responsibility.

Meeting Malaguzzi and Reggio Emilia was my first contact with the political, community and municipal dimension of education.

Later, there was also the knowledge and admiration for the quality of the environments, for the wealth of the contexts, for the opportunities – Malaguzzi often called them provocations – that were offered to the children, for the discoveries that were made together with the children and, through the dialogue of many voices, discussion and documentation became the culture of childhood.

Trying to "explain Reggio" to whose who are still not acquainted with it, I am asked questions which are a lit-

Susanna Mantovani
University of Milan-Bicocca, Italy

tle funny for us (*Is Reggio doing Vyigotskji or doing Bruner....?*) and I often answer that Reggio is "**an experience of a community that meets theories**" , manipulates them, explores them, takes them apart, makes them its own, verifies and distorts parts of them. The experience of Malaguzzi is rooted in the civic tradition of Reggio and developed from this and from politics. Malaguzzi come into contact with women who, as soon as the war was over, immediately thought of building – physically, with the bricks of the buildings that had been destroyed – a school for the children of the community: he found this an extraordinary experience, followed it, became passionate about it and became its very soul. This experience also contributed to his political commitment, which took a definite stand but which was always accompanied by free and critical thinking.

A commitment to the *left-wing* ; I use these words and I remember one episode : many years ago, at a conference in the United States, a late American colleague, Greta Fein, suggested – whilst I was talking about municipal services for children in Italy – that I should not say *left* but rather *progressive or liberal*. No, in the case of Malaguzzi it really was about being left-wing, a clear commitment to the parties of the Italian left-wing, at a time when after the anti-Fascist resistance and the war, the harshest spirit of Marxist tradition encountered and came into collision with the humanist, critical and open left-wing, the left-wing of dialogue, of which Malaguzzi was always an authoritative and awkward representative, never restricted by ideologies or party discipline but always on the side of the left.

Malaguzzi discovered the possibilities children have of activating the resources of the community and at the same time discovered with intellectual curiosity, the enjoyment of a man of the theatre and an artist's eye, the possibility that children's intelligence has in a dialogue of construction, invention and learning.

The general intellect and the social brain, wrote Marx in his Grundrisse[1] sociologically translating the Hegelian "spirit" are an immediate productive force; the collective intellect, through dialogue, generates ideas. These readings and philosophical-political suggestions which were not unusual in the cultural climate of the Italian left-wing in the post-war years were certainly present in Malaguzzi's culture, allowing him to immediately perceive the psychological and pedagogical plausibility of the so-called social constructivism.

Once again a humanistic and political culture and an experience encountered childhood, pedagogies and psychological theories. Just as the cultural and artistic sensitivity contributed to developing in the experiences in Reggio their increasingly refined evolution to make the voice of the "hundred languages of children", that

were being discovered, heard, without ever losing the political attention rooted in the local government[2] in the council-run nursery schools.

I do not think that Malaguzzi can be understood if we do not take into account his constant attention to each **individual** and together with the **network**, to the **system** whether it is a school in the schools system or an educator in the group of educators, a parent in the group of parents or a child in the group of children and this dialectic is intellectual and political.

Malaguzzi, jealous and proud of his Reggio schools, was an incredible creator of networks, a constructor of connections between systems: between schools, between towns, between the experiences of council-run schools (traces of them can be found in the places and in the memories of many educators) but also amongst all those who, nevertheless, were interested in discussing and innovating, always protecting the local Reggio identity, the *ecological niche* and at the same time capable of listening and thinking globally if this meant broadening perspectives, crossing frontiers but never drowning local identities and specificities in an indistinct uniformity.

For this reason he always spoke of the "schools of Reggio" or even of the "Diana school" or of "Villetta" or at the most of a *Reggio approach,* but never of something that was systematized, of a model or of a method. It is not possible to reproduce or to standardize, but it is possible to build up from the community, with rigour, always thinking of the *best* for children. Children, all children are entitled not just to a school, but to the best. He could not stand the idea of *minimum standards* for services and schools, because children had to experiment and have extraordinary experiences in their childhood years to try out all their potential, to keep these experiences as a foundation of confidence and energy for the future, to be able to remember them in the future with joy and with pleasure. It was the duty of the whole community to guarantee and maintain this right for its youngest citizens.

My second encounter, in greater depth and of common work with Malaguzzi was in the preparation of the Conference of the Emilia e Romagna Region *The child as a source and subject of rights,* in 1975 . Children have subjective rights as children, today, to schools of quality and it is far more important to guarantee this right than to *measure* (and how can you?) the effects of

---

[1] pages 392, 403,586,594 Italian edition by Enzo Grillo, Florence, La Nuova Italia, 1970.

[2] And it is in the *civic tradition of the local councils* as the American sociologist correctly pointed out in his book *Making Democracy Work* , translated into Italian as *La tradizione civica nelle regioni italiane*, Milan, Mondadori 1996.

this experience tomorrow. This was a subversive position for the experts in infant education who continue to ask what the long-term effects of the experience in the crèches and nursery schools will be. This position is culturally widespread in Italy – infancy is a period of life which has a value in itself and therefore there is the right to the quality of the experience, not to produce effects – of which Malaguzzi was a suggestive and provocative interpreter, refusing that the experiences of children and schools were the object and not the subject of research and debate, thus anticipating the trend of qualitative and interpretative research which seeks meanings rather than measuring standardized performances.

The best for children could be offered only through enthusiastic, rigorous and well-educated teachers, trained in an original manner through art, the theatre, photography, the new technologies and who were passionate about their schools and working with the children with the mind, eyes and hands (because "hands think" as Malaguzzi used to say) doing extraordinary things such as to arouse the surprise of artists and academics, who started to come in genuine pedagogical pilgrimage from all over the world, which in turn became a new form of intercultural training and study. Malaguzzi did not write systematically, thus avoiding objectifying his thought and experiences in a definitive and closed way; he maintained that written language is only one of the hundred possible languages and perhaps not even the best to account for the extraordinary versatility and expressiveness of the world of children and their school: he was a man of words, actions and theatre or poetic writing, estranged from the classic pedagogical production which, although he knew it very well, he filtered and was able to appreciate if he found in it thought, knowledge of children and creativity. He left articles, declarations, interviews, brief essays, poetry and even a book for children: very many traces, apart from the places and schools he contributed to creating and the rigorous method of work, open to innovation but without superficially following fashions, which is collaborative and dialectic and now continues and is developed in those who are carrying on his intuitions. But these traces have to be found, followed, discovered and reconstructed and therefore actively generate new traces. I believe that the development of new projects and new technological languages is an example : he did not introduce them but the way in which they are studied, manipulated, developed and modified creatively has much of him in it.

We are remembering him today in Reggio and all over the world, speaking about him, projecting images, writing and evoking the suggestions, intuitions and doubts that he had and that he aroused. But we remembered him only once in an Italian university, in Milan in 1995.

Malaguzzi had a difficult and controversial relationship with academic pedagogy, or rather academic pedagogy had a difficult relationship with him because he was neither respectful of it nor was he a slave to it. I remember that shortly before he started the first magazine, Zerosei, Loris came to Parma where I was then doing research and went to other universities to seek contributors. I accepted but I was advised against it because it was not an academic initiative and it was an adventure that might not please those who were working on the same subjects at the university . However, Italian academia, which often judged him too distant from "scientific pedagogy" overlooking and at times ignoring his experience, was to have to reckon with Malaguzzi in order not to become ridiculous; it was to have to measure up to a person who became a worldwide phenomenon and who has to be known, studied, interpreted and understood. Malaguzzi was a strange man who, to be a pedagogue, observed the cultural and local situation, but above all, *he would observe children:* how eccentric and what an anomaly! Malaguzzi observed children, spied on them, thought about them, studied, planned, discussed and then observed children again. And he enjoyed himself and found them "extraordinary". He was very far removed from those who only thought without getting their hands dirty, like many who do not intend wasting their time in schools, who have to apply theories, "doing" Piaget or Vygotskij. Domineering but always ready for dialogue, diffident but irresistibly attracted by what was new, by culture and art, always infinitely curious and attentive to children – "let's put in probes," he would say, "let's spy on them" because children and especially little girls are extraordinary" – and the result were books like *Tenerezze*.

The scientific paradigm focused on the study of complexity of today, of its roots in the past. of its unfathomable projections into the future disturbs and creates confusion but forces us to think. The subject of complexity was very congenial to him, the complexity of today that has its roots in the past and in tradition but which is continuously renewed; the relationship between art and science and namely the nexus between creativity and rigour is one of the distinctive features of his working method: the confusion and chaos that generate ideas and creativity are a good thing, he used to say, but they have to be manipulated and dealt with using great patience, depth and rigour. Science can dance with art, said Sergio Spaggiari and the name of one of the work groups at this conference – *the poetry of digital technology* – is an example very much in the style of Malaguzzi.

Malaguzzi, and this is another inexplicable act for those who observe our system from the outside, was not even invited to sit on the Commission that wrote the Guidelines for Nursery Schools in 1991. Out of stupidity, out of jealousy, out of fear? I still wonder why today. Because he was left-wing, but he was not aligned with official pedagogy, not even with that of the left – he was in fact one of the first to dialogue and collaborate in the local situation with Catholic schools – because he was an awkward figure who did not accept compromises with the base when children were involved? He was irritated but not surprised, nor did he invest great hopes in the commission. In the end, he recognised that it had reached a fair level, perhaps even the best level of mediation possible, but angrily and nostalgically protested because the child, the "child constructor" was not yet sufficiently acknowledged as an originator and as a protagonist.

Through political experience, in communities through his humanistic culture, Malaguzzi discovered children: "Impossible is a category to be reconsidered", he said recalling the first schools created by women after the war, "if a group of women can create a place for children out of destruction, this is an exciting anomaly, an invention that I like very much".

Children, women and politics: Malaguzzi loved women, he appreciated their capabilities and their femininity which he considered a great value. I remember the shy but affectionately intense way he spoke, even in the last years of his very long relationship with his wife, I remember the attention he showed to his collaborators who owed it to themselves and to the children, in a coherence of attention to aesthetic qualities and culture – personal care as a right and as a model: "No, the meeting can't be on Wednesday, he would say seriously, because Carlina has to go to the hairdresser's". He would look at you with an inquisitor's eyes and say "Yes, you look fine", because it was important: only by looking fine and feeling good can you make children feel good. These were the words of the demanding, implacable, perfectionist worker who was always rigorous in refusing all shabbiness because care is culture and method and children are entitled to respect, beauty and culture as essential elements in a context that makes it possible for them to shape the things, rather than children being shaped by things.

Today, remembering him, we are in the face of new challenges and I want to mention two which worry me and which I feel very strongly about. The *challenge of time*, the struggle against acceleration, against fast children ; the children that Malaguzzi observed were deep children, children with the time to think, to reflect, to discuss, to look for things and to create. We have to defend the school from acceleration and keep it as a place of formulated experience, of possible thought and reflection and, why not, of poetry and dreams, so that children can grow up not with their heads full but with their heads well made, as Edgar Morin reminds us, and so that they can relish beauty and discovery and discover and create.

The other challenge is that of interculture. Malaguzzi would have dealt with it seriously and with immense curiosity, like a new anomaly or extraordinary invention and explored it in all its possibilities. With delicacy, determination and vigour. Not defensively, residually or simply out of solidarity. With optimism and with an anthropological, human and political study because the challenge of the encounter and dialogue between culture and the intellectual transformations that dialogue inevitably creates are an extraordinary human opportunity for creation and communication. Today he would provoke and spur on all the politicians, especially those of his side, saying "Come on!".

These are some of the challenges that must make us feel nostalgic for the future, which is why we are here in Reggio today.

Thank you and Happy Birthday, Loris.

crossing boundaries

attraversar confini

Table of contents